THE KIDS' GUIDE TO LIVING ABROAD

BY MARTINE ZOER
ILLUSTRATED BY MICHELLE CHRISTENSEN

Foreign Service Youth Foundation

Acclamations for Kids' Guide to Living Abroad

"Every parent considering or preparing their children for a posting abroad should give them this book—after reading it first. As author Martine Zoer so aptly puts it, 'Moving to another country is indeed a big deal. When children can hear that the overwhelming feelings they have are perfectly normal, and then, have those feelings validated by their own peers as the many stories in this book does so beautifully, it will help establish a positive view about the relocation from the get-go. I wish this book had been available when I was moving my children abroad!'"

Robin Pascoe
Author, "Raising Global Nomads:
Parenting Abroad in an On-Demand World"

"I'll be recommending this book to every global family I work with. The voices of the kids are authentic, interesting, compelling, and reassuring. The FAQs and tips add the perspective of the wise pathfinder. A wonderful new addition to my bookshelf!"

Anne P. Copeland, PhD
Executive Director, The Interchange Institute

"What an enormous difference it would have made had my sisters and I had this book when we were growing up globally! Organized by topic, it offers story after marvelous story in the words and from the experiences of internationally mobile children themselves. There's no better counsel than that which comes from peers who've taken the journey first, and this book offers children exactly that—from the moment of being told about the move, to saying goodbye to friends, to being the new kid in school, to eventually moving on again. I recommend that all parents moving their families abroad read this book with their children and so start the kind of family dialogue upon which a successful relocation is founded."

Barbara F. Schaetti, PhD
Principal Consultant, Transition Dynamics

"I thoroughly enjoyed reading this book. The children's comments are very realistic and should be helpful to any young person who is faced with moving either from the United States to or from overseas, or from one overseas location to another. In my work with international schools, I talk with kids often and hear these very same things. This book will be a valuable resource for all families who are in a transient lifestyle. Mainly, kids reading these comments will feel like they are not alone—there are others with the same feelings about moving."

Connie Buford
Regional Education Office, Office of Overseas Schools,
U.S. Department of State

"This book takes the novel approach of seeing the experience through the eyes of kids. Zoer takes us from that exciting, but often awkward, moment of being told of the move, through farewells, settling in to the new environment, the harsh realities that follow the honeymoon period to further farewells as one moves on again, either home or to another new environment.

Although written for kids, this is also a book that parents should read, so that they can understand better the issues their children are likely to face and, by being more attuned, ease the adjustment process both for themselves and their children. By so doing they will ensure that the whole family enjoys to the full the rich, invigorating experience of living in a country and culture different to their own."

Richard Tangye
Executive Director, Council of International Schools

"*The Kid's Guide to Living Abroad*" could not be more timely. The book is packed with examples of children recalling personal experiences, good and bad, of their first move overseas. For children about to embark on an overseas life the opportunity to read about the real experiences of others is invaluable and provides them with a touchstone to guide their own preparation. The importance of parents helping their children to prepare and adjust to a new life in another country cannot be overstated and here the book is a great help.

"*The Kid's Guide to Living Abroad*" is likely to find its way onto the bookshelves of many international schools. School Directors, counselors and teachers will find this an excellent resource to share with parents and children."

Charles Gregory
Director, International Schools Services

The Kids' Guide to Living Abroad

By Martine Zoer
Illustrated by Michelle Christensen

Published by the Foreign Service Youth Foundation

Foreign Service Youth Foundation
PO Box 39185
Washington, DC 20016 USA
www.fsyf.org

ISBN 13: 978-0-9658538-4-2
ISBN 10: 0-9658538-4-5

Printed in the United States of America

Library of Congress Cataloging-in-Publication Data

Zoer, Martine.
  The kids' guide to living abroad / by Martine Zoer ; illustrated by Michelle Christensen.
    p. cm.
  ISBN 0-9658538-4-5 (pbk.)
  1. Children. 2. Children--Travel. 3. Visitors, Foreign--Handbooks, manuals, etc. 4.
Cross-cultural orientation. 5. Intercultural communication. I. Christensen, Michelle, ill.
II. Title.
  HQ767.9.Z64 2007
  910.83--dc22

                              2007010693

DEDICATION

This book is dedicated to all children who are growing up across the border. A big thank you goes out to all the young people who wrote to me about their lives abroad. I was overwhelmed by the response to my request for contributions. I wish that I could have included every single one of your submissions in the book. I am grateful to each and every child who took the time to write. I know that it wasn't always easy. The stories and the children behind them were my inspiration throughout and the reason for this book. I would also like to thank the parents and the teachers who encouraged the children in their lives to sit down and write. I know that many provided the young authors with the encouragement and the help they needed to finish their stories. I also extend my appreciation to the Foreign Service Youth Foundation (FSYF) and especially to Melanie Newhouse for believing in this book. Without Melanie and FSYF this book would not have been published. I am deeply grateful to the Una Chapman Cox Foundation and the Nelson B. Delavan Foundation. Finally, I would like to thank my husband for making my life an adventure.

Martine Zoer

Table of Contents

FOREWORD BY RUTH VAN REKEN 8

INTRODUCTION BY MARTINE ZOER 9

PART ONE: THE JOURNEY BEGINS
Moving Where? Getting the News.................................... 13
Once Upon a Time... And so the Adventure Begins............................... 17
Singing the Packing Up Blues.................................... 22
Until We Meet Again. Saying Goodbye.................................... 26
Time to Hit the Road, Air or Maybe Even Sea!.................................... 30

PART TWO: NEW BEGINNINGS
Moving into a New House 37
Around the Block in the Neighborhood 42
New Kid at School.................................... 46
The Gift of Gab. Learning Another Language.................................... 51
Friends Make the World Go Around 55

PART THREE: DISCOVERING NEW CULTURES
Loos, Ques and Chopsticks: Learning New Habits 61
Go with the Flow. Celebrating Local Holidays 66
Fashion Flair for International Couture. Different Clothes 71
Sushi Burgers and Mopani Worms: Foreign Food 75
Help, I Think a Baboon Just Ate My Shoe!! Exotic Animals 80

PART FOUR: SETTLING IN
Weathering Mother Nature. Adjusting to a Different Climate.................................... 87
Life on a Compound 92
Jumping into New Hobbies and Interests.................................... 96
Hospitable Hosting of Relatives and Other Guests 101
Family Vacations in Your Host Country 105

PART FIVE: THE REALITIES

Homesick at Home...113

Happy Birthday to ME!! 117

Pen Pals, Blogs and Text Messages. Staying in Touch 122

Sick Days 127

Visiting the Homeland..131

PART SIX: THE JOURNEY CONTINUES

Mentoring Other Kids 137

Migrating Season: Saying Goodbye to Friends.......................141

Moving Schmoving, Here We Go Again!.................................146

Identity Crisis at Age 13? Repatriating 150

Blessings in Disguise. Reflecting on the Experience 155

ABOUT THE AUTHOR

ABOUT THE AUTHOR...160

ABOUT THE ILLUSTRATOR

ABOUT THE ILLUSTRATOR..160

FOREWORD BY RUTH VAN REKEN

If you have discovered that you are about to move across the world with your family or if you are already overseas navigating your way through foreign adventures, make sure you read this book!! It tells you what you can do to help yourself enjoy all the different parts of your experience. I wish I had had this book when I was a girl moving between the United States and Nigeria or when I returned to live in the United States.

Growing up in different countries enriched my life in many ways. The world and all that was in it opened up to me. I experienced it firsthand while many of my friends who remained in the United States only read about it in books and newspapers. I ate mangoes instead of apples. The wonderful smell of harmattan (or dust in the air from the Sahara desert) took the place of snow at holiday times in the winter months. I saw the ruins of the Coliseum in Rome when I was eight years old, took a ski lift ride up the Alps in Switzerland a year later, and at age ten, waved to the Queen of England when she drove by our home in Nigeria. What a wonderful life! I had a great family and special friends and extended family in lots of places.

Even though I would not trade my experiences for anything in the world, parts of my life left me feeling sad and even angry. Leaving my grandma, aunts, uncles, and cousins in America always made me sad. The crazy thing was, however, I felt equally sad to leave my friends in Nigeria when I moved back to the United States. Sometimes I just wished I could gather my whole world and all my friends and family into one place so I could enjoy them at the same time.

Saying goodbye to places and people I loved was hard. An even greater problem was that I did not understand that my feelings were normal. I thought that I was the only one who had mixed feelings when it was time to move. I did not know that other kids and grown-ups were scared to go to new places or meet new people too. Sometimes I wondered what was "wrong" with me because I felt all these strange ways.

These are only a few of the reasons why I want you to read this book! When you do, you will discover what I wish I had known when I was young. Unfortunately I did not have this book when I was growing up. I am so glad you have it now! Have as much fun growing up abroad as I did!!

INTRODUCTION BY MARTINE ZOER

Moving to another country is a big deal. You leave behind all that is familiar and trade it for the unknown. And while it's adventurous, it is also a little scary. Before the move, you wonder what to expect. Once abroad, you have to start all over again. You have to adjust to a different house and explore an unknown neighborhood. You also have to go to another school and make new friends. You might even have to learn a foreign language.

Luckily you are not alone. Lots of children live abroad. Some live abroad for a little while. Others spend their entire childhood in another country. Children who live abroad have lots of interesting experiences. They have plenty of stories to share about their adventures. It's these stories that you'll find in this book. Amelia lives in France. She writes about learning a new language. Tyler lives in South Korea. He writes about getting used to a different climate. And Lili lives in Malawi. She writes about trying the local food.

If you live abroad, you might see yourself in these stories. Do you get homesick from time to time? Have you discovered a different hobby since moving abroad? Are you excited about going on vacation in your new country? These are the true experiences of the children in the stories in this book. This book doesn't just contain stories. It also offers advice. The advice comes from children who live abroad. The children in this book hope that you enjoy reading about their experiences. They also hope that your life is filled with lots of adventures and so do I!

PART ONE

THE JOURNEY BEGINS

Moving Where?
Getting the News

Y ou will probably never forget the day your mom and dad dropped the bomb: you were moving to a foreign country. While other people move to a new house fifteen minutes away or maybe even another state, you found out that you would be moving to another country. Why not move to Mars? For obvious reasons, you may be shocked. As your parents put a positive spin on the big move, you feel that your world is falling apart. Soon you will be trading in your familiar life for an unknown future. All sorts of feelings come flooding in. You are scared and excited at the same time. Will you like your host country and your new life? One thing is certain. From now on everything will be different.

Name: Isabelle
Age: 12
From: United States
Lives in: Singapore

"My life was perfect. I didn't have a single complaint. To me, my life was heaven on earth. I had great friends and was on an excellent soccer team. Things couldn't have been any better. It was about six weeks until Christmas. My last soccer game of the season was 30 minutes away. I daintily slid my shin guards onto my skinny legs and smacked the dirt off my old leather cleats. The leather was cracked and worn to remember the shape of my tiny feet. I hopped down the stairs.

"Mom!" I shouted, "I'm ready to go!" "Honey, can you come here for a minute?" mom's voice echoed from the kitchen. "Dad and I want to tell you something." I expected them to tell me that my game had been cancelled or that so and so had invited me over after the game. What they actually told me stayed with me for the rest of the day.

As I walked into the kitchen, my cleats clunked against the tile floor. My parents were happily sitting at the kitchen table. Their forced smiles gleamed in the light. Three or four books titled *Singapore* were stacked in a pile on the wooden table. "Singapore?" I thought to myself. "What's Singapore? Is it an undiscovered state? Is it a mall?" I was so confused.

"Isabelle," my mom started slowly. "Yes," I said, getting a little anxious. "Honey, we're moving to Asia!" my dad blurted out. Everything went silent. Everything froze. My life stopped. The world started to spin. My ship sunk. My bubble popped. This couldn't be happening. A-S-I-A. The word repeated itself in my head. I had no idea what to do. Should I throw a fit? Should I be cool about it and go to my soccer game? Why me? Why our family? Why now that my life was just right?"

Name: Phoebe
Age: 10
From: United States
Lives in: Italy

"When I got the news that we were moving to Italy, I was totally caught by surprise. My dad told us in a restaurant. I was scared and also a little happy. I had no idea that we were going to move. I wanted to know more about the country and about what it would be like to live in a city.

The first question I asked was whether we were going to live in Italy forever. The answer was no. My mom said that we were going to stay for three years and then we were going to move back. My next question was which school we were going to attend. My dad answered that we were going to go to an American school.

After that I had many more questions. My parents answered all of them. I didn't always like the answers. I wondered about our friends and family, our babysitter, and our house. The answers were that we were going to leave our family and friends, as well as our babysitter, and sell our house.

That was hard for me to hear. I was really close to all of them. It was completely hard to say goodbye. Saying goodbye to my family was the hardest. It was practically impossible. I had to leave them in the United States and would only get to see them now and then. It was hard for me to adjust to the reality. We were moving and I couldn't stop it."

Name: Michelle
Age: 10
From: United States
Lives in: Zambia

"My dad is an HIV/AIDS researcher. Because of my dad's job, I knew that we were going to move some time. One day my dad got offered a job in Africa. I wasn't surprised about the move but about the short notice. The news came in an e-mail from my dad. It came while we were on summer vacation at my grandparents' house in Hawaii.

Later my dad called to talk with each of us. He called all the way from Zambia, where HIV/AIDS is a huge problem. It was while he was there that he was offered a job. Except for my dad, none of us had been to Zambia before. I didn't even know where it was until my dad showed it to me on a map.

My dad also showed me books about the country. When I learned that Victoria Falls was in Zambia, I became very excited. I was extremely excited to go to a place I had never been before. My parents and brother had lived in Africa before I was born. I always wanted to see it for myself because I was born right after they moved back to the United States.

I saw lots of pictures of huts and thought that we might have to live in one too. That worried me a little. Luckily I found out that we were going to live in a nice house. The people who lived in the house sent us pictures by e-mail. I was relieved that I wouldn't have to live in a mud hut. By the time we moved I kind of knew what to expect. I even knew what my new school would look like because I looked it up on the Internet. I went pretty well prepared."

Moving Where? Getting the News Q&A

How am I supposed to feel about this news?

Any way you like! Finding out that you are moving to another country may feel like a bucket of cold water dumped over your head!! Emotions come pouring in. One minute you are excited. The next minute you are scared and an hour later you are as mad as can be. However you feel is fine. Your emotions are not your enemy. They help you come to terms with what is happening to you.

Why are my parents doing this to me?

Your parents are not moving to hurt you. They do not want to make you feel bad. The decision to move abroad was probably difficult for them. People move for lots of reasons. Some go because of work. Others go to broaden their horizon. Ask your parents why you are moving to another country. Once you know the answer, it will be easier to understand their decision.

Does this mean my life is over?

No! Your life does not end as soon as you cross the border. Beyond the boundaries of your own country lies a world that is waiting to be discovered. Embrace the chance to get to know another place and another culture. Tell your parents about your doubts and fears. It is important for them to know how you are feeling. Only when you open up, can they help you get through this challenging and exciting time.

REAL LIFE TIP

While it may feel like your life is over, it's not! Think of the move as an exciting adventure to anticipate rather than something to fear. Try to think about what you will gain from this move, not only what you lose.

✩Once Upon a Time...
And so the Adventure Begins

Moving to another country involves a lot of preparations. You have to get a passport and sometimes a visa. Depending on your destination, you might also have to get immunizations. All these tasks take time. They have to be done weeks or even months before departure to ensure everything will be finished by moving time. One thing you can do to prepare is to find out as much as you can about your new country. Once you know more, moving might not feel as scary.

Name: Kathryn
Age: 13
From: Canada
Lives in: China

"One day I went up to my mom and said something that would change my entire outlook on the world. This is what I said: "Mommy, I have lived in this house all my life and I want to have adventures like they do in books!" Some time later I got my adventure, but it sure wasn't what I expected at all.

My dad started looking for a teaching position in another country. Then one morning I awoke to the words "I got a job and we're moving to China." I was so excited! I had only been in Canada and the United States. I had daydreamed for years about traveling to another continent and now it was really going to happen. When I told my class at school they were pretty excited too.

My excitement was mixed with nervousness. Since I was only seven years old, I had no idea what to expect from China. I tried to prepare myself. I read books and watched movies. I liked them but they didn't tell me what it was really like to be there. We first moved to Changsha. Then we moved to Guangzhou. Changsha was far less western than Guangzhou. There were only about 200 foreigners in the entire city. My sister and I were the only foreign kids.

I thought that people in China wore traditional clothes and lived in buildings with pointy roofs. When I got here, I realized how foolish it was to think that China would be traditional. The Chinese live in apartments and wear normal western clothes like jeans and T- shirts. Yes, there are some traditional buildings, but they are temples or museums and not homes."

Name: Anna
Age: 11
From: United States
Lives in: Ghana

"My friends were very startled when I told them that I was moving. Wouldn't you be if one of your best friends told you that he was moving to Africa? To get ready for the move I did a lot of packing. It wasn't that hard to decide what to pack. I just stuffed everything I thought I would want or need for a year into a bag. It worked pretty well. It was about the least stressful packing plan I had ever gone through.

This is what I am glad I packed or didn't pack. First of all, I am glad that I didn't bring my *Gameboy*. It is so easy to get trapped in an American bubble. You could live here just as if you were in the United States. You could be totally American. But then, why live in Africa? If you're going to live as an American, do it in America.

Also, I am very glad that I brought my MP3 player. I cannot do my homework without good music. I do wish that I had brought more stuffed animals. I only brought Skip, my stuffed duck. I get homesick and with just Skip it's hard to sleep.

I am glad that I didn't bring many clothes. Here, you can buy clothes at a very reasonable price. The best thing about them is that they're not American clothes but African. The most important thing that I learned about Ghana before moving was that it was a very friendly country. That helped make getting ready for the move easy. My advice is to have fun with it. Soon you'll be halfway across the world."

Name: Marina
Age: 9
From: Puerto Rico
Lives in: Italy
Also lived in: United States

"When I found out that I was leaving Miami, I thought my life was over. I was nine years old and had lived in the United States for seven years. I loved living in sunny Miami. It was terrific. I loved my friends and my big house with its lovely pool. I also loved the sunny weather and the beautiful flowers. Now I had to leave it behind.

Everybody was really impressed that we were moving to Italy. I wasn't because I was sad. I had never been to Milan and didn't know what to expect. I prepared for the move by watching two movies. One movie was with Lizzy McGuire and the other with Mary-Kate and Ashley. Both movies took place in Italy. After watching them, I felt lots better. Rome looked really cool and they talked a lot about ice cream, which they called *gelato*.

Then the moving company came. They packed everything except the ping-pong table and the pool. It was so sad. It took four days to pack everything. When they were done we walked all over our empty house saying goodbye. I said goodbye to every room. After that we went to a hotel for a week. The hotel was close to my empty house.

The day before I left my friends from school gave me a goodbye party. First we went to a beauty parlor. We wore make-up and got new hairstyles. My hair looked like that of a flower girl at a wedding. After that we went to a Greek restaurant. We danced all over the table with a belly dancer. It was so much fun. I promised to stay in touch with my friends.

The next day I got on the plane. I knew I was going to cry and I did. Everybody did. It took fourteen hours to fly from Miami to Milan. After we landed, I was very excited. I was happy that the sun was shining. The city looked really old, but nice. I am still happy, but it was difficult. I have good days and bad ones too. I try to always be happy. I also have some news. Next summer we are moving again. Can you believe it? The only thing I get to keep forever is my e-mail address."

Once Upon a Time...
And so the Adventure Begins Q&A

Why are my parents excluding me?

Moving abroad is a lot of work. Your parents have many things to take care of and many decisions to make. Because there are so many decisions, your parents sometimes feel overwhelmed and seem to forget that they are not the only ones moving. If you want to have more of a say, let your parents know. They may not realize you want to be involved. Tell them that you feel excluded and remind them that you are moving as a family. And while there are certain decisions only adults can make, there are plenty of ways in which you can participate.

How can I help?

In a million small ways! Ask your parents what needs to be done and how you can help. Not only does it show that you are interested, but your parents will likely appreciate the help. Moving abroad is so overwhelming that your parents might feel tired and stressed. After all, even parents are only human! While most jobs might not be exciting, you will feel great to be part of the move.

What can I do to prepare?

You can prepare for your move by learning more about your host country, so that you have a better of idea of what to expect. You can also prepare by enjoying the time you have left. After all, times flies and you will be gone before you know it. Now is the time to look around and enjoy all your favorite things one more time.

> **REAL LIFE TIP**
> Stay in touch!!! Make a list of all your friends. Write their e-mail addresses and phone numbers behind their names. You also might want to write down their birthdays.

Singing the Packing Up Blues

Moving to another country requires packing and more packing. Everything needs to be sorted and put in boxes. Unfortunately, not everything can come. You have to decide what to take and what to leave behind. You also have to pack a suitcase to take on the plane. Packing is real work. Each day more things disappear in boxes until one day, nothing is left. As you look around the empty house, you realize that this move is really happening.

Name: Bevan
Age: 11
From: United States
Lives in: New Zealand

"The last time we saw our possessions in the United States, they were being loaded on a purple truck. That was my favorite color at the time. The next time we saw our possessions in New Zealand, they were on a red truck, my new favorite color!

When we decided to move, we noticed we had way too much junk. We held two huge yard sales. Then we started calling movers. Some of them didn't even know where New Zealand was. When we heard the prices, we decided to do it ourselves.

We found lots of free boxes at the recycling center. We had to get inside the dumpsters to get them out. We tried to buy some boxes, but they were too expensive. So we went back to the dumpsters. We did a lot of dumpster digging.

We had a huge metal shipping container delivered to our house and started packing. My dad built a plywood sub floor in the container to keep things dry. He said it was just in case too much moisture collected in there. We worked for days to fill the container with our furniture and boxes. Every box had to be labeled and numbered for customs. Then the purple truck came to pick up the container. We locked it up and send it on its way.

First the container traveled by truck to the railway. Then it went by train to the seaport and by ship to Hong Kong. There it changed ships and came to New Zealand. Finally the red truck picked the container up and brought it to our new house. Boy, were we happy to see it!"

Name: Vanessa
Age: 10
From: Australia and Thailand
Lives in: Vietnam

"It took a while to pack. I wanted to take everything, but I wasn't allowed. I had to take as little luggage as I could. It wasn't fair. I brought my most important things. I brought my letters, scrapbooks, books, and pens. Others things had to be left behind, including some special things, because my parents thought they were junk. I had to leave my paint pots, cardboard, and all my favorite art things. These things were special to me and I wanted to keep them.

I wanted to keep the family of butterflies that I had painted and cut out. I wanted to hang them on the wall. My parents said that I could make them again so I didn't bring them. Leaving special things like that made me mad, but I understood and calmed down. It took a very long time to pack. I had to discuss everything with my parents. They told me whether I was allowed to take something or not. I didn't really know what to pack. It was very hard. I had to get rid of some clothes and toys. I brought some huge suitcases.

When I couldn't bring things, I felt like sneaking them in somewhere. I tried to listen to my parents when they said I couldn't bring something. I guessed that they were right. My parents had to help me pack because I wanted to put so much stuff in my suitcase. I wasn't allowed to take them because my parents thought they were junk."

Name: Kate
Age: 10
From: United States
Lives in: India

"On moving day lots of packers came to my house. Before they came, I had to go through all my books and toys. My mom gave me one big footlocker. All my important things had to fit in it. If they didn't, I had to leave them behind. I had to leave some stuffed animals with my grandparents. I also had to decide what to take on the airplane and what to pack and not see for about two months. It was hard.

Then I had to pick what food to bring to India. This had to be food I could not live without for two years. I am glad that we packed *Crystal Lite* because there is nothing like it in India. My dad had to watch the packers and tell them where to put things. We were afraid that they might squish our stuff. The house was very crowded and loud. I was glad that I was not at home when the movers arrived.

We had nothing left in the house like shampoo, soap, pillows, and sheets. We moved to a hotel where we lived for a few weeks. Since I was still in school, I had to wake up earlier because the hotel was farther away from school. Every morning I picked out my clothes from a suitcase that also had everyone else's clothes in it. Luckily the hotel had a great breakfast and I had a bagel every morning. Then it was time to fly."

Singing the Packing Up Blues Q&A

What do I need to bring?

It depends on where you are going. It also depends on how long you are staying. After all, you do not need to bring everything if you will be returning in a year or two. Besides practical items, you also want to bring things that mean a lot to you. These are things that will make you feel at home once you arrive in your new country. This could be anything from a picture of you and your best friend to a favorite stuffed animal or toy.

Why is it so hard to throw away my things?

Because you are attached to them. While some things are just possessions, other things have emotional value. These things remind you of special times in your life. Getting rid of these items is like getting rid of an old friend. When deciding what to keep, ask yourself whether you need the item. If the answer is no, ask yourself if it has any sentimental meaning to you. Only keep those items that you actually need or that mean a great deal to you.

How about the things I no longer need?

Give them away! After you sort through all your things, invite your friends over. Tell them that they can pick anything they like. Your friends will enjoy having something to help them remember you. Give the leftover items to charity or hold a yard sale. That way, all your once loved things will find a great new home.

REAL LIFE TIP

When you can't take your pet, ask a friend or loved one to take care of it. While it's a lot to ask, it's worth a try. Once you know that your pet will be well looked after, it will be easier to leave it behind.

Until We Meet Again.
Saying Goodbye

Saying goodbye is tough. It is even harder when you are moving as far away as another country. You will want to say goodbye to many people. There is your best friend, your favorite teacher, and your beloved grandparents. Even thinking about leaving them behind makes you sad. You know that you are going to miss them all and wonder when you will see them again. As you give each other one last hug, you promise to stay in touch. After all, you are never too far away to send an e-mail or a letter.

Name: Sonya
Age: 12
From: New Zealand
Lives in: Bangladesh

"Leaving my country was a complex mixture of feelings. When I said goodbye, sadness was the strongest emotion. As a farewell, my friends and I were going to do something quiet. At least that is what I thought. It all began when my friend Christa invited me to stay at her house overnight. The next day we were going to have a final get together with all our friends to say good-bye.

When the night came I was all geared up for a long and final session of girly gossip. Before going to her house, Christa dragged me about town running all sorts of errands. We finally ended up at Emma's house, as Christa needed to drop something off. This all seemed normal until I was asked to wait out on the porch. At this point I began to feel a little suspicious.

I stood outside the house for about 15 minutes before I was finally called inside. I entered and was shocked to see balloons and streamers hanging from the walls and ceilings. Without warning, all of my friends jumped out at me from behind pieces of furniture. I gazed around bewildered and stunned. Then I burst into tears of surprised joy.

We partied and gossiped all night. We only got about two to three hours of sleep. And even though my face held a cheerful smile, inside a large sagging feeling engulfed me. I could only think of the fact that I wouldn't see my best friends for two years.

My last day came and more tears were shed from all of us. I looked around and saw the sad faces of my friends. They were quiet but had teardrops on their cheeks. As we said our final goodbyes, one thought kept running through my mind. Would we really be able to stay close friends from so far away?"

Name: Caitlin
Age: 8
From: United States
Lives in: Iceland

"My parents thought that it was a good idea for me to have a party before moving to Iceland. I also had the party because we wouldn't be in the United States for my seventh birthday. It was nice to have a party before leaving because I had a chance to see all my friends before I left. When I saw all of my friends sitting at the table, I wondered what it would be like to have new friends in Iceland.

We went to a 'paint your own pottery' place for my birthday/going-away party. It was really fun as we got to paint our own pottery. I picked a unicorn. I painted it to look like a happy unicorn with lots of colors. I took the unicorn to Iceland with me to remind me of home. After I put it on my desk, I looked out the window. I saw a cloudy sky and wondered whether it would ever be warm in Iceland.

When I look at my unicorn, I think about my party and about all my friends. Sometimes it makes me feel homesick. We are all settled in Iceland now. We go to cool places and I have friends from many countries. My friends are from countries such as Germany, Norway, and Canada. It was sad to leave the United States, but I am glad that I had a really good party. I still remember it today. I often think about my next farewell party."

Name: Hannah
Age: 10
From: Malaysia
Lives in: Vietnam

"When I first found out that I was moving, I was very surprised and upset. I cried because my life had gone from perfect to upside down. I felt like I was sitting on a cloud when suddenly a lightning bolt hit the cloud, making me lose my balance and fall off.

When I left Malaysia, I got to say goodbye twice. The first time was just before we moved. The second time was when we flew back to Malaysia for a birthday and farewell party that I shared with my brother. For my party, I invited most of the girls from my fourth grade class. We swam together and had a big lunch.

In addition to a party, I also spent one day in my old school. I went to all the classes I would've gone to if I had stayed. I felt very happy that I got to have two farewells. I had my first party when most of my friends were still on their summer vacation. By the time I had my second party, they were all back.

Seeing my friends in person and talking to them about my move made me feel better. I was glad they knew that I hadn't moved because I didn't like them. I wanted them to know that I would miss them a lot and would never forget them. If we hadn't gone back again, they might have thought that I didn't want to see them.

At first, I thought that Vietnam was going to be a lot different from Malaysia. I was very used to Malaysia and knew that I would miss it a lot. Once we moved to Vietnam, I realized that it wasn't much different from Malaysia after all. After a few days I had made friends and felt like I was back in Malaysia with my old friends again. I was back on the cloud."

Until We Meet Again.
Saying Goodbye Q&A

Why is it so hard to say goodbye?

Because it hurts to be without the ones you love and perhaps not knowing when you will be able to see each again. When you live in different countries, you will not be able to drop by to visit whenever you like and you may not see each other again for a long time. In addition, moving abroad is a GIANT life transition. Your entire world is changing. Not only are you saying goodbye to the people you love, yet also to the places you know. Moving to another country means that many things are going to change. And while change can be a good thing, it is a little scary.

How about leaving without saying goodbye?

While it might sound like a good idea to leave without saying goodbye, it is not. Leaving without saying goodbye will not take away the loss and sadness. In fact, you might feel worse later because you did not say goodbye. Leaving behind the ones you love hurts whether you say goodbye or not. It is because you love them that it hurts so much. So instead of disappearing without a trace, tell your loved ones how much you care.

What can I do to make it easier?

Celebrate! Even though leaving makes you feel sad, now is the time to party. Instead of thinking about how much you will miss your friends, celebrate your friendships. Have fun. Talk about all the great times you shared and create one more memory together. Ask your parents to take a picture of you and all your friends so you have a reminder of your time together.

REAL LIFE TIP
Don't forget to say goodbye to the places you love. After all, you are not just leaving behind people. Spend some time visiting the places you love most. Take a picture or bring a little memento, such as a stone or a shell.

Time To Hit The Road, Air or Maybe Even Sea! Making the Trip

Traveling to your new country may take a long time. The length of the trip depends on your departure point and your destination. Some trips may require changing planes several times and stopping to sleep in a hotel. Other trips are only a short distance. No matter how long your trip, traveling is exhausting. The wide open spaces and hour after hour of sitting still in a seat create boredom on long trips. Be sure to get enough sleep and bring activities, snacks and books. After arriving, you may suffer jetlag. Luckily, jetlag only lasts a few days. Before you know it, you will be as good as new.

Name: Nolan
Age: 12
From: United States
Lives: Croatia

"We took our cat to Croatia with us. She had to get a lot of shots and a microchip. The chip helps the vet track her down if she gets lost. We didn't know that her cage needed to have holes on all four sides. Our cage didn't have holes in the back and we had to wait for an employee to come and drill three holes in the back. It took almost an hour.

My favorite part of the airplane ride was the take-off. The plane went very fast and the engine was very loud. After lift off the ground became very far away and the cars looked tiny like toys. My brother and I watched movies on the little screen on the seat in front of us. They had all the newly released movies.

Some people brought laptops, *IPODs*, or *Gameboys*, which provided plenty of entertainment. Other people brought books and magazines. The food on the airplane wasn't very good. I think it's better if you don't expect it to be good. There is no need to be scared of flying. If you are, try not to be. Airplanes are a thousand times safer than cars.

The landing was fun. We dropped about 30,000 feet before we landed on the runway. It was thrilling, but only for a few seconds. When I first saw

Croatia, I didn't really know what to think because I was still in the airport. When my cat came off the conveyer belt, she was meowing like crazy and her hair was all spiked. I quickly took her off and comforted her.

Since my dad works at the Embassy, the Marine driver picked us up in a big van and took us to our temporary house. I sat in the front seat and thought that Croatia was quite a nice place. I think it's fun to explore new places and I hope you do too. I hope you have fun wherever you are going and that my story has helped."

Name: Chloe
Age: 10
From: Canada
Lives in: United Arab Emirates

"We left Canada on New Year's Eve. We locked up the house and went to the airport. Our cats were too old to travel so we left them with my mom's friend. My grandparents drove us to the airport and my aunt came too. When we got there, I felt kind of sad. I looked around and said goodbye to everything including the trees and the snow.

After we checked in, I went to get a bagel. On my way back, I took a penny out of my pocket and walked up to the wishing fountain. Then I turned around, made a wish, and threw the penny. Splash! I turned around to see that it had landed right in the center of the fountain. Suddenly I felt all my hopes rising.

I ran over to my family because they were getting ready to go. When I got there, they were already giving each other hugs and saying good-bye. Grandma was trying not to cry, but she couldn't help it. Then we went through all the stuff that we needed to do like security. We flew first class to London. On the way we had a quick stopover in Newfoundland. We celebrated the new year on the plane.

When we arrived in London, we had fun. Even though I have been there before, it was still exciting. They use pounds in Britain but that's ok because every year my great aunt sends me money from Wales. We bought some yummy toffee at a store in the airport. After waiting in the airport, we got on the flight to Dubai. I watched a movie. It was exciting.

When we arrived in Dubai, everything seemed different. When I stepped outside, it wasn't cold or hot. It was just right. Then we drove to our friends' house. We stayed with our friends for three weeks while mom and dad decided on a villa. I started school pretty soon after we arrived. I've made lots of new friends. Dubai isn't that hard to get used to, once you know how!"

Name: Jules
Age: 8
From: Australia
Lives in: Cambodia

"I found out that I was moving while at my grandparent's house in Sydney. One day my mom jumped out of bed and said "Jules we are going to Cambodia." I didn't want to go and told my mother. I told her that I didn't like Cambodia. Mom said that we were going anyway. I told her that it wasn't fair.

Then my mom told my sister Sabine. Sabine said that she loved Cambodia. I growled at her and stuck out my tongue. I asked my mom if we could stay in Australia. She said, "No, we are going and that's that." I got my cousin to come over and told him all about it. He said that I was very unlucky.

A week later we got a taxi and went to the airport. We did all the stuff we needed to do and got on our plane. My dad wanted to go to Cambodia. I felt sad and a little angry. When the plane landed Sabine asked when we were going to get to Cambodia. My mom said that we had to take another plane.

I felt a little better on the second plane because I was able to sleep. I like planes you can sleep on. When we got on the second plane my sister didn't look so good. An hour later she threw up. The next morning we arrived in Cambodia. We stayed at a hotel and started going to school. My teacher was called Mr. Warren. At the end of the school day, I said, "I love Cambodia."

Time To Hit The Road, Air or Maybe Even Sea! Making the Trip Q&A

What should I expect?
It depends on where you are going. Some trips only take a few hours. Others can take a day or even more. Most trips involve a trip to the airport and a flight. During the flight, you may feel a little sad. This is especially true if you've just

said goodbye to your loved ones. Try to look forward to the adventures and experiences in your future. You also can write about your feelings in a journal or diary.

How do I pass the time?

Bring something to do. While taking a long flight might sound exciting, the thrill soon wears off. After a few hours on the plane, being confined to your seat is no longer much fun. To make time go by faster, try taking a nap. If that doesn't work, watch a movie, listen to music or read. Bring activities that don't take up a lot of space. Comic books, IPODs and small games are perfect for long flights.

What is jetlag and what can I do about jetlag?

As you travel across the world through different time zones, your body's internal clock will be knocked out of sync. These disruptions in time differences can cause you to feel tired, disoriented and you may have an upset stomach. Some jetlag is almost inevitable. To lessen the effect of jetlag, take care of yourself before and during the flight. Eat healthy food and drink lots of water. Also make sure that you sleep properly and exercise. When you're healthy you'll be able to recover from jetlag faster. In a couple of days, you'll be back to your old self.

REAL LIFE TIP
Expect to be bored! All long flights drag on, no matter how much stuff you bring. Try to sit back and relax, knowing that in the end you'll arrive at your destination.

PART TWO

NEW BEGINNINGS

Moving Into a New House

Moving to a different country means moving into a new house. Some families have a new house or apartment waiting on arrival. Other families will stay in temporary housing for a while. This could be a house, an apartment, or even a hotel. While staying in temporary housing can be fun, you will be glad when you finally move into your own house. Soon the moving company will bring your belongings and you will have your own space again. Now, all you have to do is turn a house into your home.

Name: Adriana
Age: 11
From: United States
Lives in: Italy

"I remember walking out of the car to see a medium sized apartment building. As I walked through the door I almost missed the elevator because of my jetlag. My mom steered me in the right direction. The elevator smelled faintly of cigarettes.

As we rode up, my parents talked about the era the elevator was from. Suddenly it stopped and gave a jerk. I lumbered through the door into the apartment. My old house was in the suburbs and had a yard. I loved nature and needed a lot of space. Our new apartment looked too small for our family of five plus a dog and a cat.

While my sisters explored our new home, I was about to collapse from exhaustion. I briefly looked at the entrance hallway and listened to my parents go on about the beautiful floors. I then asked where my room was and fell asleep on the bed.

Many hours later I woke up. It was afternoon, but it felt like morning. I slowly roused myself and went to find my mom. I searched the apartment and found her in what turned out to be the kitchen. I didn't realize that it was the kitchen because the fridge was in the hallway.

"What's today?" I asked thinking that I had slept through the night. My mom said it was the same day. She told me I had slept for six hours straight. I was hungry and glad that my mom was cutting bread. She brought me into the hallway and I sat down at the kitchen table. I wondered why the table was in the hallway along with the fridge.

My mom handed me a piece of bread. I asked for some butter, but she looked at me like I was mental. I wondered if I was still sleeping. My mom explained that they don't use a lot of butter in Italy. After I got over the shock, I sighed and ate my bread. I could tell it would be a long time until I could eat like an Italian."

Name: Binaramalie
Age: 11
From: Sri Lanka
Lives in: Bangladesh

"The night we arrived at our new house, I was really tired. It was early January and cold outside. My father came to Bangladesh before us. When we arrived, he showed us around. I looked around the apartment and thought it looked very small. I was tired and did not think about it too much. I quickly fell asleep.

The next morning I still didn't feel that well. I was excited about exploring our apartment. I looked around the house carefully. All I saw was an empty apartment. Our new house was nothing like our house in Sri Lanka. Our old house had two stories and a huge garden. Our new house was an apartment and there was no sign of a garden.

When I looked again, I saw some plants and also some furniture. The apartment was not that empty after all. I still concluded that there was really nothing that exciting about our new place. So then I went to help my mom unpack our luggage. Even though, my mom already had started unpacking, I wanted to give her a hand.

It wasn't easy to unpack. We had to give everything a place. It was also hard getting used to the cold climate and the environment. It took me a whole day to settle down and get used to the new apartment. I felt like I was trapped in an unknown place. Eventually I got used to the place and after a few days the apartment felt better."

Name: Adelaide
Age: 9
From: United States
Lives in: Malawi
Used to live in: Russia and South Africa

"I have never lived in one place for more than two years. One of the best parts about moving so much is getting a new house every time I move. In Russia, I lived in a two-story compound. The houses were so close that from my balcony I could touch my friend Emma's balcony. This was the first time I ever had my own room.

Each time we move, I only bring one suitcase. Empty closets can make great playrooms but I still miss my stuff. When the big shipment comes, it's like Christmas. I use boxes and anything I can find to make forts. It's so much fun playing with things I haven't seen in a while. I also like organizing my room. We always take our furniture. It's a little weird to see the same set of furniture in all these different houses.

After Russia we moved to Cape Town, South Africa. I had so much fun exploring this house and yard because it had a pond. I not only had my own room but I had my own playroom. We even had a guestroom and a huge kitchen. From my room I had a beautiful view of the mountains. Right now I am living in Malawi. We've lived in two houses since moving here. Our first house was huge. It had about twenty different rooms and was a little creepy because it also had rats. My mom didn't like rats and so we had to move to a different house.

Our second house is the one I live in now. It is very nice but kind of small. There are only a few rooms and it's cozy. I decorated my room with big paper flowers that I made myself. I put a string-like curtain in my doorway that I love to walk through. My favorite part of the house is the tire swing outside. Overall I love all the houses that I've lived in. I like to move around a lot. It's always an adventure!"

Moving Into a New House Q&A

When will we move into a new place?
Soon! When first moving abroad, you might have to stay at a temporary place for a while. This could be a hotel or even an apartment. While staying at a hotel is fun for a little while, it soon becomes tedious. Try to enjoy yourself. Watch TV from the bed or swim in the hotel pool. When you get bored, remind yourself that this is only temporary. Before you know it you will have a house again.

Why don't I like my new house?
Because it is not your old house. Getting used to a new house takes time. Loving your new house takes even longer, particularly if you enjoyed living in your old house or if you lived in your old house for your entire life. Sometimes a new house is bigger, sometimes smaller. Other times, the style or architecture

of the building differs. Just because it is different does not mean that you won't enjoy living there. Give your new house a chance. Once you get used to it, you might actually like it.

Will this place ever feel like home?

Yes! There is a big difference between a house and a home. A house is where you live. A home is where you feel … well, at home. It takes time and effort for a house to become a home. You can make yourself feel comfortable and connected to your house by decorating it with your favorite things. You also can make an effort to enjoy your house and your family. The fastest way to make a house into a home is by creating special memories.

REAL LIFE TIP
Bring a special item with you wherever you go. It could be anything from a picture of your best friend to a favorite toy. This will help you feel at home no matter where you are!

Around The Block
in the Neighborhood

Arriving in a new country may awaken an explorer inside you that you had no idea existed. Investigating a new neighborhood is a great way to expand your horizons and learn about your new country. While it is fun, you also may find it confusing. Every country has its own way of putting a neighborhood together. While some neighborhoods are carefully planned, others evolved over time. Your new surroundings may seem strange to you. At first, everything about the new neighborhood may seem all wrong. Maybe you used to live in the mountains and now you live near the sea. Or perhaps you used to live in the country and now you live in the city. Adjusting to this new world may take a long time. Luckily it will also make exploring more fun.

Name: Derek
Age: 10
From: United States
Lives in: Croatia

"I live in Zagreb, Croatia. Our neighborhood is big, but not too big. My brother and I have a friend who lives a few houses down the street. We usually play with him. He's twelve and has a little brother who is six. We've got two soccer fields. They are both within a mile of our house. Luckily soccer is my favorite sport. My brother's favorite sport is basketball.

The kids in Zagreb are good at soccer. In Croatia soccer is called *futbol* and football is called American football. There are a lot of little stores where I can buy Coca-Cola and other drinks. There are only a few fast food restaurants here like McDonalds and Subway. There is no Taco Bell and no Burger King. Lots of people in Zagreb start their own businesses. I guess they have some money in the bank after all. I didn't think so because they have so many apartments here. I think the government built these apartments after the war they had ten years ago.

The money here is called *kuna*. Fifty *kuna* is worth ten dollars and that's my allowance. The laws aren't as strict as in the United States. I haven't seen many police officers patrol the street. As a matter of fact, I haven't seen many cops at all. One bad thing is that I have to be careful when I cross the street. Everything else is okay. For instance, my house is kind of big. I've got a big downstairs to put all my toys and video games. It's easy to see that my neighborhood has many things for kids to do and is a good place to live."

Name: Jacqui
Age: 10
From: Australia
Lives in: Norway

"I've just moved from Australia to Norway. I now live by a fjord south of Oslo. From my house I can see the fjord. Every two hours a ferry goes past my window. My neighborhood is called Asnes. It's a suburb of the town of Sandefjord, which has thirty-five thousand people. This is very big compared to all the towns I've ever lived in Australia.

In my new neighborhood I can ride my bike to all the houses because it's not far. I also go swimming off the granite rocks. When I go swimming, I have to look out for jellyfish. I can also go crab fishing. One time I caught thirty crabs with a piece of string and a clothes peg. Down by the beach there is a German bunker left over from World War Two.

In Australia, I used to live in a country town called Naracoorte. It was between South Australia and Victoria on the road between Adelaide and Melbourne. I lived 100 kilometers inland in a farming area that was quite flat. Around town there were wheat crops, sheep, and vineyards. My house was two kilometers out of town on a large block.

I used to see native animals near my house. I saw echidnas, kangaroos, and lots of birds. There were also venomous snakes. I always had to be on the lookout for them. Across the road from my house, I could see native bush land. This is where many more animals lived like snakes and lizards.

I only moved to Norway this summer. I think that the main difference is going to be the snow. Where I lived in Australia, there was no snow at any time of year. During the winter the days are going to be short here too. I'm not looking forward to getting up in the dark."

Name: Anja
Age: 11
From: South Africa
Lives in: Oman

"Hi. My name is Anja (pronounced Anya). It's not an English name. You see I am from South Africa. My house in South Africa was quite big and had a massive garden. Then I moved. I've moved before so I am quite used to it now. This time I moved to Oman. This move was different because Oman is in the Middle East. The biggest change was the heat and humidity.

When I got to Oman, I was eight years old. At the airport my aunt and uncle were waiting for us. We got in the car and they took us to our new house. It was empty and hot. I was sleepy and went straight to bed. I slept until twelve the following afternoon. After I finally woke up, I took a shower. It was hot again, but the water was nice and cold. I still wished it was colder. I wished it was freezing cold.

After lunch, I explored the house, the garden, and the neighborhood. I met one of the neighbors. He had four dogs. Three of the dogs were big and one was a little puppy. The big dogs were black and the puppy was white. The big dogs went with the neighbor to work. The little one stayed home. He was all alone and I went to visit him every day. A month later it was my birthday. My neighbor gave me the puppy. I named it Max. That was the happiest day of my life."

Around The Block
in the Neighborhood Q&A

How am I supposed to find my way around?
Finding your way around a new neighborhood can be challenging. The best way to figure things out is to explore. Make it fun by involving the whole family. Take a walk or drive with your parents. Look around to see what there is to do and discover the short cuts and best routes. Before you know it, your new neighborhood will be just as familiar as your old one.

What if I can't find my way home?

Don't go out by yourself until you feel confident that you know your way around. Once you start going out by yourself, make sure you know your address. You should also memorize your phone number. That way you can call home or ask for directions if you get lost. If you have a hard time remembering your new address, write it down on a piece of paper. Make sure you take it with you wherever you go.

Where are all the other children?

You may be surprised to discover that the children in your new neighborhood do not play outside. There are no kids riding bikes up and down the street and no kids in the park playing basketball. Maybe this is because it is not safe or maybe because it is not part of the local culture. Of course the children in your new country do play. Try asking around to find out where the other children go to play. It could be that they play at school or at each other's houses. Once you find out where the other children play, you can talk to your parents about going there too.

REAL LIFE TIP

Think of your new neighborhood as a series of circles and you live in the bull's eye. Start by exploring the smallest circle, which includes your house and immediate surroundings. Make the circle a little bigger each time you go out. This way you will explore your new neighborhood one area at a time!

New Kid at School

First day of school jitters are as common as kids who love pizza!! When your first day of school is in a foreign land, the butterflies in your stomach may seem more like a bunch of rocks. When you go to a new school in a foreign country, you have to learn more than just math or reading. You may have to learn an entirely new language and new rules. Your school may include students from all over the world. With so many changes all at once, you may feel overwhelmed. While it may take you a little while, eventually your new school will feel just as familiar as your old one.

Name: Lucy
Age: 11
From: Ireland
Lives in: Belgium

"It was 6:50 in the morning. My alarm blared. I turned it off and sat up in bed. I was going to tour my new school today, and I didn't want to go at all. I worried that I would get lost and not know anybody. When we drove up to the school, I discovered I had been right. It was huge. There were about ten buildings.

We found the tour for the English-speaking parents. It was led by a man with a very quiet voice. No one could hear him. My mom said that the man spoke like a mouse. I didn't care because I wasn't listening anyway. I was looking around the group trying to spot children that would be in my class.

I saw a tall man with his ear pierced. He had his hand on a dark-haired girl's shoulder. She looked about my age. I wondered who she was. When the tour was over my mother said that we'd be going to my classroom to meet the teacher. I hadn't thought about that. My teacher! Oh no! What if he was really mean and horrible?

Mom took me to a red brick building called 'The Gutenburg'. I was surprised that they named the buildings. They never did that at my old school. My mom told me that Gutenburg was the man who invented printing. I realized then that they named the buildings after people. I wondered if there was a building named after Britney Spears.

I forgot all about this when we reached the door of my classroom. I could see through the door and saw a middle aged man talking to some parents. I found out from the name on the door that his name was Mr. Black. "Mr. Black?" I laughed. "Does he have a friend named Mr. White?"

Mom opened the door. All the parents stopped talking and stared at us. Mr. Black asked who I was. I told him that my name was Lucy. Even though Mr. Black sounded friendly, I was shaking. He suggested that I sit down. He pointed to a desk with a girl sitting at it. I sat down next to her. "What's your name?" I asked. "Aifric," she replied with a smile. "I'm Lucy," I said.

We ended up chatting until the end of the lesson. We had a lot in common. We both liked books and were both from Ireland. I looked across from me and saw the dark-haired girl. Aifric and I leaned over and asked her what her name was. She said it was Catriona. Both girls were really nice. I've been going to my new school for three years. Catriona and Aifric are still my friends."

Name: Tariq
Age: 12
From: Oman
Used to live in: Norway

"I moved to Norway from Oman because my father had some work to do there for four years. First we lived in Kristiansund for two years. Then we moved to Stavanger. In Stavanger, I went to my very first elementary school in Norway. I was seven years old and they put me in third grade.

I was lucky because my friend Mohammed stayed and helped me. Mohammed was also from Oman. We were supposed to go straight to our class when we arrived. They told us to buy indoor shoes and outdoor shoes. When we were inside the school we wore sandals and when we had breaks we wore trainers.

My very first lesson was English. The teacher said everyone's name. I was trying to remember them all. I hoped that the other students would be my friends. Our teacher's name was Miss Davies, but we called her Miss D for short. Our lesson was to draw our friends' faces and talk about them. I drew Mohammed's face as a Chinese face and he drew mine as a monkey face.

The days and terms passed by and I made many friends. My best friend was William. He was the worst behaved student. He taught me bad words. My next best friend was Guilliame. He was a good friend because he made me laugh. He also invited me to his house and his parties. One time we went on a field trip to an island. It was so much fun. When we arrived it was late and we were shown to our rooms in the dark. Guilliame and I had to pee real bed. The next day we had both wet our beds. Then it was time for me to go back to Oman. Now I really miss Norway. I miss my school and I miss my friends."

Name: Roshni
Age: 11
From: India
Lives in: Bangladesh

"Three years ago, my father was transferred to Bangladesh. We looked at various schools for me and my sister. My parents thought about putting us in the International School of Dhaka. So we went to check it out. I was very impressed with the school but thought that the buildings looked weird. They looked different from the buildings in my previous school.

I also met with some of the teachers. They were very friendly. Then the head of primary school took my sister and me to the huge library. We took our test there. Later I joined third grade. My teacher was strict but funny. On the first day of school I was scared and excited. In class I felt very lonely because I had no one to talk to or play with.

At lunchtime I saw some girls playing. I wanted to join them but I was too shy to ask. The next day some girls sat with me at lunchtime. They started to talk to me and I felt very happy. A few days passed and these girls became my best friends.

The system at my new school is different than the one at my previous school. At my previous school we had many subjects. We also had books and homework. At the international school we don't have many subjects. We don't have textbooks either. Instead we use worksheets. At my previous school we didn't have a cafeteria. We brought lunch from home and ate it in the classroom.

There were no school buses at my previous school and we had an assembly every day. During assembly we had to sing the national anthem or the school song. At the international school we have only weekly assemblies. Until grade five we didn't have much pressure to study. Now that I am in grade six, we have to study a lot. I am completely at home in my new school. In fact it doesn't feel like a new school any more. I make it a point to be kind to new students."

New Kid at School Q&A

I am really scared to go to a new school. How can I prepare?

Have an open mind and a sense of humor. The only sure thing about going to a new school is that things will be different. It's easier to deal with these differences if you are open to them. Try not to compare everything to the way things were done at your old school. Look at new things as discoveries. After all, just because something is different does not mean that it's better or worse. If you can, visit your new school before the first day of classes. That way you find out if there are any special procedures. You also get to see your classroom and maybe even your new desk. Also find out what the other kids will be wearing and try to dress similarly.

What if I get lost?

Ask for help! Not knowing your way around your new school can be a little intimidating. It is easy to get lost if you do not know your way around. Plenty of other students have gotten lost before you, so there is no reason to be embarrassed. Just remember that everyone at the school was a new student once and that teachers are teachers because they love kids!! If you do get lost, just ask for help. Other students or teachers will be happy to point you in the right direction. Before long you will be the one helping new students.

Why don't I understand what is going on?

There can be many reasons. Perhaps you do not understand the language well enough. Or maybe the curriculum at your new school is different. It could also be that there are cultural differences. Whatever the reason, let your parents, school counselor and teachers know what is going on. Find out if your new school offers programs for new students. This could be anything from an orientation to extra language lessons. Taking advantage of these programs is a great idea!!

REAL LIFE TIP
Check out the afterschool programs and clubs. Your new school may have lots of interesting sports and activities. A new school always offers you the chance to try out cool new things.

The Gift of Gab.
Learning Another Language

People around the world speak many different languages. In fact, there are 6,912 living languages!! Chances are that the people in your host country have a language that is different from your own. While you can still use your own language at home, it is a good idea to learn the local language. This will enrich your time abroad and allow you to communicate with the local people. Learning a new language is tough. At first, the words seem strange and the grammar nonsensical. Luckily the more you practice, the easier it gets.

Name: Amelia
Age: 10
From: United States
Lives in: France

"I live in Paris and go to a French school so that I can learn the language. My first year was very difficult. I couldn't understand what the teacher was saying and everything was very different. We wrote with fountain pens and wrote the date backwards. We wrote the day first and the month second. We used notebooks with lines like a grid. There was no school bus. I had to go to school on the metro train.

Now I am in my second year. We still do all these things, but they don't seem so strange anymore. I now know what the teacher is saying and I can communicate. French is pretty hard to learn, but in some ways it's similar to English. Some words are alike in French and English. For example different is différent, dessert is dessert, and salad is salade.

I had special tutoring to help me with my French. Vocabulary is the toughest for me because it takes time to learn words. I know more words in English than I do in French. My favorite thing about French is conjugating verbs. I discovered that I'm good at it. The best thing about knowing French is that I can talk with and understand all the kids at school. Plus I can enjoy everything in Paris. It doesn't matter if a movie or a show is only in French, because I am able to understand it.

This year at school I am also studying German. I've never spoken German before, so I am in the beginner's class. I think it is fun because we sing German songs and my teacher is nice. Some of the words sound like funny English. When I learn a new language, I have to work hard. I make mistakes, but that's okay. I learn from my mistakes."

Name: Nasreen
Age: 8
From: United States
Lives in: Saudi Arabia

"When we moved to Saudi Arabia, I had to learn a new language. It's called Arabic. It has a different alphabet and you write it from right to left instead of left to right. In the morning I have Arabic class for three hours. Learning Arabic was a little hard at first. It helped that I started school here in the first grade and that my grandma only speaks Arabic. Now I'm in the third grade and it's a lot easier.

I can talk to all my friends. Some of them speak only English and some of them speak only Arabic, but most of them know both languages like me. It also helps to know Arabic when we go out to the store. Some people speak English. There are also a lot of people who don't understand English. We need to use Arabic with them. At home we speak English. I like to read books in English from the library."

Name: Iseabail
Age: 8
From: Scotland
Lives in: Spain

"I first thought that learning a new language was scary. Now that I know more words, it's much easier for me. The first Spanish word I learned was hola. It means hello. Then I started to have lessons with a lady called Yvonne. The lessons helped me an awful lot. I needed to learn a lot of Spanish because not many people here speak English. Only one boy and one girl at my school know English.

The best way to learn a language is to play with new friends. I played with children who spoke Spanish all the time and didn't speak English. It was easy. Most of the games were the same so I just had to learn the new word for them. When I got things wrong, my friends didn't laugh at me. They helped me.

I know much more Spanish than my parents. So does my sister. My sister and I like to say things to each other in Spanish that our parents don't understand. At school I take Spanish lessons, but I know most of the lessons already. That is because we moved here before the summer vacation. I had a lot of time to learn. My friends in my old school gave me extra Spanish lessons. They taught me many words and those words were very important.

My mom helps me with my homework and I can read and do math in Spanish. When I am twelve I will go to the big school where I will learn French. I will be able to speak three languages. That is a really good thing because I can go anywhere in the world I want to. It really is pretty fun and easy to learn a new language. It helps if you try hard and are not shy about trying it. Adios!"

The Gift of Gab.
Learning Another Language Q&A

What if I make a mistake?

Don't stress! Everyone makes mistakes. It is not a question of *if* but *when*. Try not to worry about making mistakes. It is part of the process. Other people will understand. Don't let the fear of making mistakes stop you from trying. The biggest mistake when learning a new language is giving up.

Why is it so hard?

Because learning something new is always hard. Learning a new language is no exception. The only way to learn anything is to practice. After all, like the saying goes, 'practice makes perfect.' Try not to compare the language you are learning to the one you already know. Each language is unique and comparing only makes it harder. You can also try to make learning enjoyable. Practice your language skills by watching TV or reading a book. That way you will have fun while you learn.

What if I forget my first language?

You won't. Just because you use your first language less, doesn't mean that you will forget it. The first language you learn is so deeply rooted that it is impossible to forget, even if you try. It is, however, possible for your language skills to deteriorate. It's a good idea to keep up with your first language. This is especially important if you will return to your country at some point. Try reading books in your first language. You can also write letters or e-mails to friends and family back home.

> **REAL LIFE TIP**
> Be patient. Learning a new language is hard so try not to get frustrated. Instead of focusing on the things you don't know yet, focus on the progress you have made.

Friends Make the World Go Around

At first you may feel lonely while living abroad. You have just left your friends behind and don't know many people yet. Even though you want to make new friends, it may not be easy. It's even harder if the other children seem different or speak another language. However, don't let that discourage you from trying. After all, having friends is one of the best feelings in the world. Once you get to know the other children, it will no longer seem so scary to make friends. Just give it some time and before long, a new group of friends will surround you.

Name: Hadley
Age: 8
From: United States
Lives in: New Zealand

"It took a long time to make friends here, but eventually I did. I am home schooled, so I can't make friends at school. There are a lot of boys in our street. My brother is friends with all of them. I am friends with them too, but I would still like to have a girl living close. I used to have a friend living right across the street from me when I lived in the United States.

I made friends with a lady in our neighborhood. She has a dog. I met her when she was out walking her dog. I see her around the neighborhood. Every now and then I pick some flowers for her. I take them to her door, ring the doorbell, and say hello. I joined Brownies and made a couple of friends there. Brownies are all over the world and it's a good place to make friends.

I am a big bookworm. I have three girlfriends and they are bookworms too. I started a book club. It's for girls only. I invited my bookworm friends to join. At my book club, we choose a book and everyone reads it. Then we get together and talk about the book. Then we choose another book. We don't live close to each other, but we have our meetings at my house. I like to plan the refreshments.

Almost everyone here speaks English. People have a lot of different accents. In the book club all four of us speak English. We come from four different countries and we use different words for things. Luckily we do understand each other. A boy on our street may be moving soon. Maybe a girl will move in. I hope so!"

Name: Muzn
Age: 12
From: Oman
Lives in: Turkey

"I was shocked when my parents told me that we were moving to Turkey. I had to pack my things and say goodbye to my cat, Nala. I was sad because Nala couldn't come with us. When I first got to Turkey I felt happy and a bit sad. I didn't know many people and didn't have any friends.

I told myself that it was okay and that I would make new friends. We stayed at a hotel. It was so hot that I decided to put on my bathing suit and go to the pool. I was about to jump in when a girl tapped my shoulder and said "hi." She told me her name was Ariana. She also told me that she was from Israel. Then she asked what my name was and where I was from. I told her that my name was Muzn and that I was from Oman.

Ariana and I became good friends. She was my best friend in Turkey. I really liked her because she was my only friend. One day my family and I went on a boat trip. It was so much fun. I saw all kinds of fish through the transparent glass on the floor of the boat. After the trip, we went back to the hotel. I looked for Ariana but couldn't find her. No one had seen her either.

I went to the pool and after a while Ariana showed up. I was happy to see her. Then she told me that she was going to leave and go back to her own county. I felt sad, really sad. Ariana went home and I was alone again. I wondered what to do now. I could either go for a swim or I could annoy my sister. I decided to annoy my sister. It was a great idea. I love annoying my sister. I like it because I have somebody to play with."

Name: Caleb
Age: 9
From: United States
Lives in: Armenia
Used to live in: Suriname

"Making new friends can be hard. It's even harder if you move a lot. I have friends from all different countries. I also have friends that are from the same place as me. Friends my age play the same games as me. It's fun because we already know the games. I don't have to teach them new things and I don't have to learn new things. We just have fun.

Some of my friends are not the same age as me. It's good to meet people of different ages. When my friends are older, they teach me cool new things. When my friends are younger, I teach them things. I like having younger friends because I like teaching them new things.

I think that making new friends is hard. Sometimes it takes a long time before I meet kids my age. When I am new, I like to explore the neighborhood to see if there are any kids around. I also look out for other people that are new. When new people arrive I like to teach them about the country. I also teach them about the other people here so that they can make friends quickly. I like bringing new people something to eat like cookies.

When I meet new kids, I ask them lots of questions. This is how I get to know them better and find out if we like the same things. I also like to find out if they like different things than me. Sometimes they like things I've never heard of but that I can learn. I like moving a lot because I have friends from all over the world who play unusual games.

I'm glad that I have a lot of friends. I get to play with them a lot. They can come over and play and we can do new things together. When I have friends, I don't get as lonely or bored. I hope that I make a lot of new friends in my next country!"

Friends Make the World Go Around Q&A

How can I make friends if I don't understand the other children?

Don't let language and cultural differences deter you from making friends. At first, you may think that these differences present an insurmountable barrier. How can you be friends if you have no way of communicating and nothing in common? First, try smiling to show that you would like to be friends. If you take the time to get to know the other children, you may discover that you have a lot in common. The other children might play the same games and have the same interests. However, it is not until you get to know them that you will find out. A great way to make friends when you do not speak the same language is a local choir, music club, art class, sports team or even the local playground.

What if no one wants to be my friend?

Take the initiative. Do not wait for other children to come to you. When it comes to making friends, you have to take charge. Approach the children that you would like as friends. Show that you are interested by asking questions. You can also tell them a little bit about yourself. Introducing yourself is the first step. Now that you have met, you can say hi when you run into each other or sit together in class.

Why does it take so long?

There are no rules about how long it takes to make friends. Sometimes you are fortunate and make a friend on the very first day. Other times it takes longer. This is because every situation and every person is different. Even if it takes you a while to make new friends, don't give up. After all, good friends are worth the wait. The next person you meet might become your next best friend.

REAL LIFE TIP
Before you move, ask your parents to help you find other children in your new country. Ask them to contact their employer or the school you will be attending. That way you can introduce yourself by e-mail. You might even make friends before you move!

PART THREE

DISCOVERING NEW CULTURES

Loos, Ques and Chopsticks: Learning New Habits

One of the best things about living abroad is experiencing how other people live. And while living in a different culture can be fun, you may be confused. There is a lot to absorb. Different languages, clothes, and behaviors surround you. Sometimes people do things that you would love to try. Other times people do things that you just do not understand. When that happens you may wonder what planet you are on. However, as you stay in the country longer, you may actually get used to these things. After a while many of the customs that seemed strange at first, no longer seem so unusual.

Name: Jason
Age: 12
From: United States
Lives in: Thailand
Used to live in: Russia, Austria, and Germany

"Upon arriving in Thailand, I immediately found out that things would be very different from the other places I've lived. The most important thing I learned is when you cross the road in Thailand, you have to be very careful. There are three main reasons. First, the cars drive on the left side of the road and not the right side. Second, cars and motorcycles generally go faster than they should on the narrow streets of Bangkok. Third, most cars and motorcycles have no intention of slowing down to let a 12-year old, like me, cross the street.

I now look carefully every time I cross the street. I look right and then left. Even at school I found myself getting trampled by other students when I walked on the right side of the hallway. In Thailand people don't just drive on the opposite side of the street. They also walk on the other side of the sidewalk.

Another problem I had was adjusting to the friendliness of the people here. That sounds odd, doesn't it? How can it be hard to adjust to friendliness? It's hard to believe, I know. When I walk down the street, every person I make eye contact with says hello. Well, they don't say hello, they say *sawadee khrap,* which is Thai for hello. At first, this kind of confused me. In the other countries where I've lived, there wasn't a single person who would make eye contact, let alone speak to me. Now I'm being greeted left and right. It can be confusing because I have to remember to say hello back."

Name: Maria
Age: 9
From: United States
Lives in: Zambia

"When I moved to Zambia, I found women carrying heavy loads on their heads. At first that was quite strange, but then I got used to seeing it. Also in Zambia the men ride bikes, while the women walk. I think it would be quite awkward for Zambian women to ride a bike because of the clothes they wear.

The local women wear a piece of brightly colored cloth that they wrap around like a long skirt. It is called a *chitenge*. They also wear T-shirts. If the women have babies, they carry them on their backs wrapped in a *chitenge* that they tie at the front. I've not tried to wear one yet.

When I heard that I was coming to Africa, I was really happy. I knew that I would see many nice animals. There are great safari parks here. They have antelopes, giraffes, elephants, and many other species of wild animals.

The local food here is *nshima* or corn. When I first tasted it, I thought it was very strange. Soon I got to like it even though it's white and a bit tasteless. Another food commonly eaten is *kapenta*, which is a very small fish. It's a very healthy food and it's eaten whole: head and all! I don't find it that good.

In the United States, I used to go trick or treating around the building. The local people here are puzzled when I tell them about that tradition. Most have never heard of Halloween. Since moving to Zambia, I celebrate Zambia's Independence Day. It's on October 24th. Many people here celebrate Ash Wednesday and Palm Sunday. I'm still not too sure what they are about."

Name: Chandler
Age: 9
From: United States
Lives in: Scotland

"My new school was very different. I had to get used to lots of new things. One thing I had to get used to was the different subjects that seemed weird to me. I now have subjects like 'topic' and 'bullying.' This year in topic we are learning about the Scottish War of Independence. On the positive side, learning can be fun. On the negative side, I doubt that I'll ever use this knowledge.

As well as new subjects, I had to get used to new teachers. The teachers here yell a lot. This is really strange to me because my teachers in the United States never yelled. Even some parents in the neighborhood yell. They aren't being mean. They just have a different way of disciplining.

The holidays here are different too. I encountered some unusual things to celebrate. Take for example Guy Fawkes Day. This is when the Scottish celebrate a man named Guy breaking into parliament and unsuccessfully trying to blow it up. On Guy Fawkes Day, they make a fake person and roast him over a bonfire. It's a fun holiday, but also unusual.

Another strange holiday is called Bank Holiday. There is at least one of these every month so we get out of school a lot. That's obviously the good part. The weird part is that I don't even know what a Bank Holiday is. I don't know why people celebrate it. I mean it's just a bank.

Another thing I experienced was communication problems. Here are some words that are different in Scotland: *pants* are underwear and *trousers* are pants. One time my teacher asked us to write an essay about our mothers. For what my mother likes to wear, I put "her greenish yellow and black pant suit." Everyone giggled. It was only later that I found out that everyone must have been picturing my mom in her underwear."

Loos, Ques and Chopsticks: Learning New Habits Q&A

Why are people acting this way?

People around the world have different ways of doing things. To an outsider, these habits may seem strange. Yet to the people, this is normal. Just like the way you behave is normal to you. Their way of behaving is their culture. At first you may notice a lot of differences, but after a while you do not notice them anymore. You may even acquire some of the habits that once seemed so peculiar.

How am I supposed to react?

It is easy to disapprove when people behave in a way you don't understand. But just because something is different does not mean that it is wrong. It is important to respect other people and not judge them for their differences. Try learning about the custom. Once you understand the tradition, you might even want to try it yourself.

What if I don't know what to do?

Chances are that there will be misunderstandings when you first take part in a new custom. When that happens to you, don't worry about it! No one expects you to know what to do. After all, the custom is new to you. Ask a local person or another child who has been in the country longer what to do. They will probably be excited by your interest and happy to explain it to you.

> **REAL LIFE TIP**
> Don't just get your toes wet!! Jump in and take part. This is your chance to experience things that you would never have experienced back home. If you are scared, ask a friend to join you. That way you have support and someone with whom you can share the experience.

Go with the Flow.
Celebrating Local Holidays

People all over the world celebrate different national holidays. Some holidays exist to commemorate something unique about the country or its history. This could be anything from a leader's birthday to the day the country became independent. Other holidays have a religious basis. These holidays are celebrated by people around the world who belong to the same religion. For example, Christians celebrate Christmas and Jews celebrate Hanukkah. Some holidays may be familiar to you but the traditions and manner in which the holiday is celebrated differs from your experience. Getting used to the holidays in your host country may take some time. It also can be fun. After all, who doesn't like a party?

Name: Sydney
Age: 8
From: United States
Lives in: Netherlands

"When I celebrate Dutch holidays, I feel part of the community. I get a bit nervous, but feel happy and fortunate to be with friends. I have three favorite Dutch holidays. They are *Sint Maarten, Sinterklaas,* and *Koninginnedag. Sint Maarten* is on November 11th. It's like Halloween except that you don't dress up. Children carry Chinese lanterns and go door to door. I made my lantern at school. At each house, kids sing a song in Dutch and get a small treat.

Sinterklaas is like having two Christmases in one month. Sinterklaas arrives from Spain on a ship in November with lots of helpers called *Zwarte Piets*. At night, you put your shoe by the chimney or on the front step. Don't worry if your shoe is stinky. Sinterklaas won't mind. You put some carrots or apples in your shoe for Sinterklaas's white horse. In the morning, you check your shoe. If you've been good, you get little presents. I like the chocolate letters and the little surprises that Sinterklaas leaves.

Koninginnedag is on April 30th. It's the Queen's birthday. On this day everyone wears orange and waves flags. It's like the Fourth of July without the fireworks. The day is also a gigantic yard sale where people sell their junk. Last year, my best friend Nadja and I decided to earn some money. We made posters to sell cookies and performed free gymnastics tricks with each cookie sold. Our sugar cookies with orange sprinkles were a hit. We sold everything. Even my teacher bought a cookie."

Name: Saskia
Age: 8
From: Canada
Lives in: Senegal

"Senegal is very different from Canada. One very big difference is that in Senegal it never snows. Even in the winter it's burning hot. Winters in Canada are freezing. Another thing I learned is that in Senegal there is a holiday called *Tabaski*.

On that holiday you have a big feast of sheep and goat. The stores downtown are mostly all closed. There are people everywhere carrying pots and pans. Even a few days after *Tabaski* there are some left over sheep tied up. Every year *Tabaski* is ten days before the day it was the year before. Africans celebrate the holiday.

People who can afford to buy a sheep share it with many other people. Our housekeeper always brings us a huge chunk. I like *Tabaski* in some ways but not in others. I like it because I get a holiday from school. I don't like it because killing the sheep is not very nice. *Tabaski* is an important family holiday. It is just like Christmas."

Name: Jasmine
Age: 11
From: Australia
Lives in: Japan
Used to live in: Malaysia

"I was nine years old and living in the exotic country of Malaysia. I had lived there for nearly a year, when the festivities began. It was late October and the festival ran until early November. Everyone around me was happy. It was *Deepavali*: the Hindu Festival of Lights.

The festival was felt in the air. As I walked through the malls, streets, and plazas there were beautiful patterns in rice laid out on the floor in exotic colors and patterns. The patterns showed images of flames, animals, and strange but amazing symbols.

At school everyone came in different brightly colored *saris* and other Indian clothing. Weeks before the festivities started each class or year prepared something to show the school. The entire school celebrated the holiday. It was so much fun.

The food that we ate was mostly sweet or traditional Indian food. We also ate food that Hindus eat. The holiday lasted for about five days. I spent my time eating, singing, dressing up, and having a great time. However, the Hindus had their own special ways of celebrating. The Hindus had lots of glowing candles in very small clay holders. I saw many images of people holding candles to celebrate the festival.

During the festival friendly cards and messages were given to people. They were colorful, meaningful, and had images of Deepavali. The cards also had 'good luck' and other messages on them. Before the festival started everyone went out to buy new clothes mostly consisting of bright colors and unique designs. No one wore black or dark colors because the festival is supposed to be celebrating light. Everyone looked colorful and happy. The festival was unlike any other that I have ever experienced."

Go with the Flow.
Celebrating Local Holidays Q&A

What are they celebrating?

Ask someone. To the people of your new country, their national holidays do not need explaining. After all, they have been celebrating these same holidays their whole lives. To you these holidays are new and somewhat mysterious. You might even find yourself with a day off from school without knowing why. Ask a friend or teacher what they are celebrating. They will probably be impressed that you express an interest. Once you know the reason for the celebration, you might even decide to join in yourself.

Am I supposed to celebrate too?

Only if you want to. This is your chance to experience the traditions of another country. However, you should only take part in a celebration if you feel comfortable. It is okay if you decide to watch from the sidelines. It is nonetheless important that you respect the people and their holidays. While to you it is just another day, to the local people it is a day of celebration or even worship. Rather than joining in, you can choose to watch from a distance. That way you get to learn about a new holiday without actually participating.

What about my own holidays?

Keep celebrating them. Your holidays are part of your national identity. Celebrating them maintains your connection to your own country and its history. You will feel closer to the people you left behind. At the same time, celebrating a national holiday while abroad can be a real challenge. It can be hard to find the foods or the decorations associated with the holiday. If you are unable to locate the required items, be creative. Try substitutions. By doing so, you put a spin on the old traditions. This will make the celebration even more special.

REAL LIFE TIP

Share your own national holidays with others. Ask your teacher if you can give a presentation about your holiday. You could also bring a symbol or goodie connected to your holiday to share with your class.

Fashion Flair For International Couture. Different Clothes

People around the world dress differently. Fashion styles and tastes may be very different in the new country. A hot fashion trend in one part of the world may be considered unattractive in another. Other times diverse climates determine styles of dress. For example, you dress much differently when you go to the beach than when you play in the snow. People also may dress in certain clothes because of tradition, heritage or because it is required by their religion. Ways of dressing change over time. Once upon a time many Dutch people wore clogs. Nowadays hardly anyone does.

Name: Lily
Age: 10
From: United States
Lives in: Switzerland

"People in Switzerland don't dress all that different from people in the United States. There are some differences. What are they? A lot of people wear the same outfit two or three times in a row. This is weird to me because many people have five different coats and only a few different outfits. Another difference is that a lot of people wear knitwear, especially in the winter. Almost all the knitwear is homemade, that is home knit.

Another difference is that the clothes kids wear don't always match. I remember a girl in third grade wearing plaid pants and a shirt with a totally different pattern. It didn't match at all. Sometimes at school I see kids wearing the same clothes as me. This is because there are fewer choices in the stores here. Most stores have the same clothes as back in the United States. Some have shirts with really cool patterns that you would never find in the United States.

They don't have a lot of malls here and I have to walk around the whole city to go to different stores. They have good things in the stores, but you can't always count on getting exactly what you want. When I am in the United States during the summer, we buy stuff there because it's cheaper. If we need something later we get it in Switzerland."

Name: Marigold
Age: 10
From: United Kingdom
Lives in: Japan

"The clothes in Japan and England are very different. Japanese people do wear some of the same clothes English people wear. They also wear traditional clothing called a *kimono* or a *yukata*. English people don't have a traditional piece of clothing although the Scottish wear *kilts*.

Japanese people wear their traditional clothing at weddings and other parties. They also wear them on the coming of age day. This is when people celebrate their 20th birthday. *Kimonos* and *yukatas* are long. They come all the way to your ankles. When wearing a *kimono* or a *yukata* you also wear special shoes. These are called *getas*. They are a little bit like flip-flops.

On casual days Japanese people wear normal clothes. In my opinion some of the fashions the girls in Shibuya wear are a little bit over the top. The temperature in Japan is very different from England. If you are moving to England, I suggest bringing lots of clothing for winter. However, if you are moving to Tokyo, I suggest bringing some trendy clothes for walking through Shibuya."

Name: Anisah
Age: 10
From: United States
Lives in: Saudi Arabia

"In Saudi Arabia people wear different clothes than in the United States. Women wear something called an *abaya*. It's like a thin robe that goes over the regular clothes. It's usually black. Women also cover their hair and their faces with a black veil. The men wear a white robe called a *thobe*. They sometimes cover their heads with a red and white scarf.

Everybody looks the same as everybody else. Sometimes the kids get mixed up about who their parents are. One time I was at a store and all the ladies were wearing black. I started talking to someone who I thought was my mom. It wasn't. It was very embarrassing.

The foreign men here usually wear the same clothes as in their own countries. The foreign women must wear the *abaya* over their clothes when they go out. The veil isn't required. Kids wear regular clothes, but girls start wearing the *abaya* when they're about ten years old.

I wear regular clothes at home, but when we go out I wear the *abaya* over them. It is black and has snaps and ties to close it. It's like wearing a long, thin coat. For school I wear a uniform. It is a long, burgundy jumper with a white blouse."

Fashion Flair For International Couture. Different Clothes Q&A

Why are people dressed like this?

That is not an easy question to answer because there are a lot of reasons why people dress the way they do. Just imagine someone asking you that question. Would you be able to answer? Some people dress a certain way because they like how it looks. Other people dress a certain way because they are required to do so because of religious reasons or because it is their uniform.

How am I supposed to dress?

It depends. Clothes express how you feel and your personality. However, you might not always be able to dress exactly as you like. Some countries have rules about what you can wear when you are in public. For example, in some countries women are required to cover their hair with a scarf. In other countries, you may be required to go barefoot. Rules like these also might apply to foreigners. In some situations, like at school, there might be a dress code or even a uniform. Dressing alike can give you a feeling of solidarity. It shows that you are on the same team.

Where do I buy my clothes?

You may not be able to find the clothes you are used to wearing while living abroad. Many families take advantage of visits home to go shopping. However, if you have just hit a growth spurt, you may not want to wait until the next trip home for a shopping spree. One solution is to shop at all your favorite stores on the internet. You also can ask other children where they buy their clothes. You might even want to try some of the local clothes. At first you might feel silly wearing a *kimono* or a *sarong*. After a while you might actually like this new way of dressing.

REAL LIFE TIP
Don't throw clothes away just because they don't fit anymore. Most countries have charities that would love to receive your second hand clothing. Not only are you able to help those less fortunate, but it feels great to make a difference.

Sushi Burgers and Mopani Worms: Foreign Food

People in different countries eat different foods. In India, you might be served a plate of many different curries and in Mexico you may eat tacos and *enchiladas*. To the people of your new country their national dishes are typical, everyday food, like peanut butter and jelly sandwiches. To you, they are exotic and exciting. It can be daunting to try these new dishes. After all, you do not know whether you are going to like them and you may not know exactly what you are about to eat. You also may crave the food that you used to eat and be shocked to discover that your favorite foods do not exist in your new country.

Name: Lili
Age: 9
From: Spain
Lives in: Malawi

"When I moved to Malawi, I was happy to see all the lovely fruit. We have a mango tree in our yard. Mangoes are orange on the inside and green on the outside. They're getting big now and are starting to fall off the tree. When we can't eat the mangoes from our tree, we buy them from street vendors. We argue about the price and buy about 50 of them. We eat them whole or cut them up. Sometimes they're still hard and we have to wait for them to go soft before eating them.

We also have a *paw paw* tree in our yard. Sometimes the *paw paws* fall or the guards climb up and cut them down with a knife. My mom cuts them up and we eat loads. They are sticky but not too sweet. We used to have strawberries in our yard but now we buy them from the vendors who come to our gate. We sometimes have them with ice cream.

In Malawi you can buy bananas all year round. Our whole family likes them especially my baby brother. We usually get some when we buy gas. My mom and I love oranges. We're so excited when they come into season and buy bags of them. We cut them up and drink the juice. When we buy a coconut we throw it on the floor to crack it. I like the huge ones with lots of juice inside. I suck the juice out with a straw. It takes ages to get it all out. When I have a coconut it makes me think of being in Hawaii.

Malawians eat lots of mangoes. The children pick them up from the ground. They also eat lots of sugarcane because it's cheap. When I eat sugarcane I understand how they make sugar. I rip off the outside, which is like soft wood, and suck the sugar from the inside. After I eat sugarcane I have to brush my teeth. I love our food in Malawi."

Name: Vidur
Age: 11
From: India
Lives in: Mexico
Has also lived in: Argentina, South Africa, and Indonesia

"When I moved from Indonesia to Mexico I was pretty ignorant about Mexican food. I knew nothing about *tacos, tostadas, nachos,* or any other Mexican delicacy. All that changed when my family got a Mexican maid who cooked all kinds of wonderful local dishes. It was the best food I had ever had.

There's a tremendous variety of Mexican food. Sometimes I have *tortillas,* which are a kind of thin, flat and round bread with meat or vegetables. Every Friday for lunch I have a scrumptious *tostada.* A *tostada* is a flavorsome, crisp *tortilla* with a topping of bean sauce and a sprinkle of cheese. Once in a while we have *quesadillas.* They are my favorite. *Quesadillas* are *tortilla* sandwiches with cheese in between and, often, other fillings.

Another type of food I discovered was the *taco,* which is heavenly. *Tacos* are crisp *tortillas* wrapped around some meat and/or some vegetables. Finally there are *nachos.* Mmmmm, succulent, delicious *nachos! Nachos* are somewhat like *tostadas* except without any toppings. They can be eaten as a side dish or as a snack.

So that's how I live my life in Mexico. I eat Mexican food nearly every day. Now you might think that eating Mexican food all the time would eventually get boring, right? Well for me it doesn't at all. I love Mexican food. *Viva la comida Mexicana!*"

Name: Avery
Age: 10
From: United States
Lives in: France
Used to live in: Japan and Cameroon

"I've lived in three foreign countries: Japan, Cameroon, and France. The people in all of these places eat some strange and different foods. I've tried some of these things, but others I've just left alone.

A peanut butter and jelly sandwich is normal to American kids. To

Japanese kids rice balls covered with seaweed are normal. They bring them to school in their lunch boxes. These rice balls are called *onigiri* and are really pretty tasty. Since Japan is surrounded by water, Japanese people eat quite a lot of seafood. They eat such things as lobsters, crabs, tuna, and salmon.

Once at a Japanese friend's house, I was served a plate with two huge crabs on it. They were looking straight at me. Being only four years old, I was terrified. That was my worst experience in Japan. The Japanese also have some very surprising desserts. When I think of dessert I expect something like chocolate cake or ice cream. The most common desserts in Japan are made from beans. I used to eat buns filled with sweet bean paste called *anpan*. There is even a cartoon about a bun-headed super hero named *Anpanman*.

In Cameroon, the people eat many interesting and sometimes disgusting foods. Some of the best fruit in the world grows there. I got to taste the most delicious mangos, papayas, pineapples, and coconuts. We even had a banana tree and a papaya tree in our backyard. There are some things that Cameroonians eat that I never tried. This includes porcupines, monkeys, crocodiles, pythons, bats, termites, and grasshoppers. Yuck!

The French are known for their food. It's world famous. They're especially known for their delicious and stinky cheese. I eat it, but I hold my nose while doing so. The French also eat snails and frog legs. I pass on those, but always take the opportunity to eat the chocolate. All countries have different and unusual foods. I like to explore the different tastes, with a few exceptions. Some of the foods that I've tried for the first time in a foreign country are still my favorites."

Sushi Burgers and Mopani Worms: Foreign Food Q&A

What am I eating?

Ask someone! All over the world people eat different foods. One group of people might consider something inedible. The same food might be a delicacy to others. If you are unsure what you are eating, just ask. If it turns out to be something you would rather not eat, don't. Explain to the person that it is not something you are used to eating. They will likely understand.

Am I supposed to eat that too?

It is up to you. Sometimes new things turn out to be scrumptious. Other times –YUCH!! It is all a matter of taste. Most people like certain foods because they grew up eating them. Take haggis for example. While the Scottish love it, other people might find it disgusting. Don't let the thought of eating something new stop you from trying it. After all, if you don't like it, you will know never eat it again.

Where can I find food from my home country?

It depends on where you live. If you live in a large city you might be able to find it in a special store. These stores carry foods from all over the world. If you live in the country, the foods you are used to might not be available anywhere. If this is true for you, ask a friend or a relative back home to send you your favorite foods. You might even try making your favorite treat from scratch. You also can pack some in your suitcase the next time you visit your home country. That way you have a stash of peanut butter or Oreos whenever you have a craving.

REAL LIFE TIP

Share your country's foods. When you live abroad you get to experience lots of different foods. In return you can introduce your new friends to some of your own favorites. Next time a friend comes over for dinner, cook your favorite national dish. That way they get a little taste of your home country.

Help, I Think a Baboon Just Ate My Shoe!! Exotic Animals

Discovering exotic animals can be fun especially if you are an animal lover. In your own country, wildlife may only live in the zoo. In your new country, wildlife can be all around you, even in your own backyard. Each time you observe a new animal, you may be tempted to try to touch it or get close. You should keep your distance. After all, even little creatures can be dangerous. When you encounter an animal on your own, get the help of an adult. They will be able to determine whether it is safe to observe the animal. They will also know when it is time to get an expert.

Name: Jake
Age: 12
From: United States
Has lived in: Argentina, Malaysia, Thailand

"In Thailand, we lived in a hotel for a while before we found a house. One stormy, rainy day something strange and gross happened. A swarm of termites came and attacked our hotel room. They flew around and around. Then they lost their wings. It was like a thin layer of snow on the carpet. The termites were crawling everywhere. My mom called housekeeping and they said they'd send someone right up. Luckily the termites died really quickly. By the time housekeeping got there, all they had to do was vacuum up the thousands of dead bugs.

There were also some really cool creatures living right beneath the bubbles on the beach. They were called sand-bubbling crabs. One day on the beach, we saw strange geometric designs all over the sand. They were perfect and all the same. We couldn't figure out how they got there. We looked at them and noticed that at the center of each one was a tiny crab. It was pretty cool and really beautiful. The crab makes that design when it passes the sand through its body to get food out.

Next to our house was a small park. It was infested with all sorts of ants. There were also clusters of leaves on the ground that looked like some sort of package or nest. One day I peeled one and tons of ants came out. I found out later that they were called weaver ants. They make those packages by sealing the leaves together. When it rained there were centipedes everywhere on our street. We used to play with them because they would roll up into big balls. It turned out that the centipedes were dangerous. One kid almost got bitten. We stopped after that."

Name: Freya
Age: 8
From: United Kingdom
Lives in: Uganda
Has also lived in: Denmark and Belgium

"I've lived abroad all my life. I've mostly lived in Europe where the most exotic animal I saw was a red squirrel. Last year we moved to Uganda and my world changed forever. We now live in Kampala. Here crested eagles sit on the electricity poles in our garden and marabou stork fly overhead.

There are cows with huge horns that graze outside our gate. There are also birds that sing from the bushes on our driveway. I have seen brightly colored lizards that sit on our wall. One day we even had a black snake outside the kitchen door. Our guard took a stick and killed it. It turned out to be a poisonous snake and even our guard was scared. Luckily no one was hurt.

Our first safari was to Queen Elizabeth National Park. The park is seven hours from home. I saw animals there that I've never seen in the wild before. I saw elephants, lions, and antelope. I also saw monitor lizards, which can swim. One lioness had five cubs. We never saw the lion. However, recently we saw a huge lion eating an antelope just inches from our car.

We also saw a cheetah resting under a bush. The cheetah is my favorite animal of all. I've seen a wildebeest migration. This is when two million animals cross the Mara River each year. Luckily there were no crocodiles that day and no lives were lost. We did see a mother zebra swim back to collect her baby from the other side.

My greatest discovery is a bird called the *shoebill*. There are only a few left in the world. There are only twelve in Uganda. One day we spotted two near the Nile. They looked like they were from the days of the dinosaurs. They were as tall as me!"

Name: Jakayla
Age: 8
From: United States
Lives in: Armenia
Used to live in: Suriname

"I love animals. I like traveling all around the world because I get to see different animals in every place. If I keep my eyes open, I see lots of animals wherever I live. When we lived in the rainforest, we saw iguanas and geckos in our yard every day. Now we live in a place that is very dry. We've had camel spiders, a viper, a scorpion, and many praying mantises in our yard.

There aren't as many animals in the city as there are in the country. If I want to see animals I go into the wilderness. I have a lot of fun exploring. I make sure we bring a camera and binoculars. When we lived in the rainforest we took many trips into the jungle. We saw monkeys, snakes, caiman, parrots, toucans, colorful frogs, and leaf cutter ants.

I always stay with my group when I go on a trip. This is very important. I don't want to get lost or be alone with unknown animals. Before I go, I read about the place where we're going to see what kinds of animals live there. I make sure I learn how to stay away from poisonous or dangerous animals. I also learn what to do if I see them. One more thing I do is keep my eyes and ears open. That way I can see and hear the animals around me.

Exploring for animals is exciting but can be scary. Wherever you live, find out about the animals in your area and prepare to go out and see them. But be careful and respectful. Then you can have a wonderful time no matter which country you live in."

Help, I Think a Baboon Just Ate My Shoe!! Exotic Animals Q&A

What's out there?
It depends on where you are. Try finding out by reading books or asking around. Every continent has different wildlife. Think for example about elephants in Africa or kangaroos in Australia. It can be really exciting to discover what exotic animals live in your country. It is especially exciting if those animals do not exist in your home country. Make a list of all the animals you discover. You can also try to find out a little more about each of them.

How do I know what to do?
You don't. When it comes to animals the thing to remember is that they are wild. People or books might give you advice on what to do. Keep in mind that this information does not always apply. Every situation and every animal is different. When confronted with a wild animal, the best thing to do is get help. After all, that harmless looking koala bear or raccoon might not be as innocent as it looks.

Can I keep it?
No. Wild animals belong in the wild. Though it might be tempting to take one home, it is a bad idea and may even be illegal. No matter how well you look

after it, wild animals do not belong in the home. You can help wild animals in many ways. You can become a member of a nature organization or volunteer for a local environmental group. That way you are helping animals without harming them.

> **REAL LIFE TIP**
> Keep an eye on your pets. In your home country, it might have been safe for them to go outside. In your host country this might not be the case. It is better to keep your pets safely inside than risk their injury or even death.

PART FOUR

SETTLING IN

Weathering Mother Nature.
Adjusting to a Different Climate

Countries all over the world have different weather. The climate depends on where the country is located. Countries close to the Arctic experience relatively colder weather. Countries close to the equator are relatively warmer. In some countries, it is so warm that people nap in the afternoon heat. In other countries it's so cold that people wear sweaters year round. Adjusting to a different climate can be especially hard if the weather in your host country reaches on of these extremes. You may also have to cope with the natural phenomena, such as, earthquakes, tsunamis or tornadoes.

Name: Tyler
Age: 8
From: United States
Lives in: South Korea
Used to live in: Australia, Egypt, Tanzania, and the United Arab Emirates

"From the time I was born, it seems that the weather was always hot, humid, or wet. Sometimes it was all three at once. What a surprise it was to move from Africa to South Korea. It was summer when we first arrived. The weather was warm but not hot like in Africa. We went to the beach for a barbecue. I ran straight down to the sea and jumped in. The water was freezing.

I was so surprised. The water in Africa was always like a warm bath. In Africa we would go swimming at the beach nearly every day. We don't swim at the beach much in South Korea. We go to a big swimming pool instead. It has hot water that comes from a natural spring in the mountains.

In Africa we had thunderstorms. In South Korea we have typhoons. Once when we were in Busan, a typhoon hit. We were in a hotel because my friends were going back to the United States. It was our last night together. We were on the 10th floor looking out onto the road. Suddenly we heard a big gust of wind. Then we saw a massive electric spark on the building across the road. The spark looked like fireworks. After it hit, all the lights in the building across the road went out.

We decided to go to the other side of the hotel. From my room we watched the waves coming in. They were so big that they covered the beach and rolled up to the shore. The water washed the sand from the beach and into the aquarium next door to the hotel. When we woke up the next day, all was quiet. We went out onto the street and saw sand everywhere. Telephone poles and flagpoles were bent over. Windows were smashed and there was glass everywhere. It was scary!!"

Name: Linu
Age: 11
From: Finland
Lives in: Germany

"I've lived in Germany for almost eight years. I no longer really notice the different climate. I do still miss the snow in Finland. Here in Germany, there is hardly ever enough snow to build a four-foot tall snowman. If I am lucky, I can make a snowman that is three feet tall. There is never enough snow to make a snowman that is six feet tall.

There might be enough snow somewhere, like on top of the nearest mountain. However, that doesn't count because I don't live on the mountain. The summers in Germany are hot. At least it feels really hot to me. In Finland the hottest it ever gets is about 30 degrees Celsius. In Germany the hottest weather hovers around 40 degrees Celsius. Last summer I felt as if I would melt right where I was standing. Luckily we went swimming on the really hot days.

Spring comes earlier in Germany. I don't mind this because spring time in Germany is beautiful. The fall is also nice. It's so beautiful. The leaves turn gold and copper and the air becomes nice and crisp. It all looks so beautiful, especially in the forest. It's just about the loveliest sight you can see. Fall is my favorite season in any country."

Name: Sophie
Age: 9
From: United Kingdom
Lives in: Japan
Used to live in: Kenya and Scotland

"I was born in Kenya in July. Because Nairobi is south of the equator, I was born in the winter. People in England tell me that I was born in the summer because in July it's summer in England. I don't remember a great deal about Kenya. I do remember that it was very hot and that I didn't like wearing shoes. I also remember that I loved seeing all the wild animals. I especially liked feeding the wild giraffes.

It was a shock to move from Africa to Scotland. It was so cold. The weather was windy and wet. I didn't like going out of the house without thick woolly clothes on. I wouldn't even have liked it if someone had paid me. It was hard for me to adjust. One minute I was in piping hot Kenya. The next I was in freezing cold Scotland. I didn't think I would be able to survive this sudden change of climate.

I now live in Japan and it's such a relief. When I arrived it was quite warm. The thing with Japan is that the seasons are really obvious. When you think about the summer, you imagine heat. Well Japan in the summer is really hot and humid. When I ride my bike I get very hot. I bring lots of water bottles in my basket ready to drink.

When you think about the winter, you imagine cold. Winter in Japan is very cold. We even have snow. Riding my bike to school in the snow is very difficult. It's slippery, but the skies are bright blue and the sun still shines. Springtime in Japan is beautiful. The cherry trees are in blossom. When the petals fall it's like cycling in pink confetti.

In the fall all the leaves change color and fall to the ground. I can crunch leaves on my way to school. The weather is at its best in the spring and the fall. During those seasons it's not too hot and not too cold. I can just wear T-shirts and shorts. I love living in Japan. I have lived here for five years. That is just over half my lifetime. I don't know where we'll move next, but I wonder what the weather will be like."

Weathering Mother Nature.
Adjusting to a Different Climate Q&A

Why can't I stand this weather?
Because you are not used to it. While living in different climates can be fun, there are also times when it gets tiresome. After all, being stuck inside because it is too hot or too cold is not fun. While you may feel miserable, acting annoyed or grumpy will not help. Instead try to make the best of the situation. When the weather prevents you from going out, have fun indoors. When it is cold, make some hot cocoa and curl up with a good book. When it is hot, sit in front of the fan with an ice cream cone.

Will I ever get used to it?
Probably! Adjusting to a different climate is another challenge. You have to give your body time to realize that you are somewhere new. It is going to take longer to adjust if the climate in your new country is extreme or very different from where you used to live. To help your body, slowly increase the amount of time you spend outside. You also should observe the behavior of the locals. They are experts when it comes to dealing with the local weather. Watch how the locals behave and copy it. If they drink lots of water and walk in the shade, do so too. If they dress in warm layers and always cover up, do the same.

What am I supposed to do?

Talk to your parents. Some countries experience harsh weather like tornadoes, earthquakes, and hurricanes. Experiencing Mother Nature's force is especially frightening if the phenomenon is new to you. Prepare for the possible event ahead of time. That way you are ready to act if the time comes. Help your parents come up with an action plan. Having a plan makes the thought of something happening less scary. It also helps you cope, just in case nature decides to show its power.

REAL LIFE TIP

Take a picture of one of your favorite places during all four seasons. Try to take the picture from exactly the same location. This way you have a great keepsake of what your special place looks like year round.

Life on a Compound

Living on a compound means that you live in a secluded area away from the local population. Within the boundaries of the compound, you do not have to stick to the cultural rules of the host country. You are free to live the way you used to in your home country. A compound has its own roads and its own houses. It might even have a playground or other facilities. Many families call the compound home. These people come from all over the world. On one street, you might find families from all seven continents.

Name: Gaby
Age: 10
From: United States
Lives in: Cameroon

"My family and I live on a large compound in a big house. I enjoy living on our compound because it's really big. It is so big that we were able to put up a basketball hoop and a trampoline. I also like our compound because I can ride my bike around the yard. We were even able to get a dog for the first time in my life. His name is Smokey.

Our compound is enclosed by walls and has a gate to let cars in and out. There is also a guardhouse where the night guard stays. On the side of the guardhouse there is a door for us to go in and out. I feel very safe inside our compound walls. On the outside of the guardhouse is a button. If you press that button a bell goes off in our house to tell us that someone is there to visit. I guess we call that a doorbell in the United States.

Inside the compound there are flowers and plants everywhere. They attract a lot of mosquitoes. Though we have many plants, we only have five small trees. Three of them are big enough to climb. We can climb two of them without a rope. We need a rope to climb the other one because it doesn't have long enough branches. One of our trees is an avocado tree and the other one is a papaya tree. Neither has any fruit yet.

Our compound is a square one. We have neighbors on three sides. The compound has four windows on the front wall. I don't always like the windows because people can see us and know that we are white. Because we are white and they are Cameroonian, they want to come in and play all the time. The other bad thing about our compound is that we can't ride our bikes out on the street. Luckily my dad made a bike path that goes all the way around the house. It's lots of fun. Other than those two things, living on a compound is great. Living in Cameroon is one of the best parts of my life."

Name: Anna
Age: 9
From: United Kingdom
Lives in: Japan

"Most of the time living on a compound is a good thing. Sometimes it's a bad thing. It's a bad thing when you want to go outside alone. It's also a bad thing when you have a disagreement with a friend. This is bad because you can't get away from everything. Another thing I don't like is that most children on our compound are younger than me.

Despite this, I wouldn't say that living on a compound is totally bad. It's nice most of the time. I like the way I can go out of the house and play without my family worrying. I also like the guards at the gate. They are very friendly and look after us.

We have many parties on the compound and lots of people come to look at the pretty cherry blossom trees. I like springtime on the compound because there are many children to play with. I also like it when everything is silent and tranquil. I find this very relaxing."

Name: Henrik
Age: 12
From: Norway
Used to live in: United Arab Emirates

"When I lived abroad, I lived in a house on a compound. There were lots of other children living there. They had all moved to Dubai for the same reason. That reason was so that their moms or dads could work. There were people from many different countries. There were a Swedish family, a Finnish family, a Spanish family, a British family, and many Norwegian families.

Living on a compound with lots of different people was fun. I got to learn a new language. I also learned about other people and how they are. Something that was really new to me was that every family had a maid. Our maid was named Mary. She cleaned the house and did the laundry. She also looked after my brother and me.

One of my best friends lived on the same compound. His name was Alvaro and he was Spanish. Alvaro was the same age as my brother. Our compound was very big. It had about 101 houses. It also had a big long wall going all the way around it. The wall was there to stop thieves.

In the middle of the compound there was a big swimming pool. There was also a bar, two tennis courts, and a playground for the younger kids. It took me quite a while to find my way around. There were so many winding roads. There were big winding roads and smaller ones. There were also little roundabouts that were decorated with palm trees and bushes.

After a while I learned that there were many different shortcuts. These could lead you anywhere. The best part about living on a compound was Halloween. I didn't have to walk across busy streets. I could just go trick-or-treating in the neighborhood. I got lots of candy because there were so many houses."

Life on a Compound Q&A

What is there to do?

It depends. Most compounds have some facilities like a playground or a clubhouse. Larger compounds tend to have more facilities. Some even have a swimming pool, a gym or a tennis court. One way to find out what there is to do is by exploring. Another is by asking the other children. They might be able to give you a tour. Before long you too will know all the shortcuts and the best places to hang out.

Why do people live here?

Different people have different reasons. Some live on a compound for safety reasons. Compounds are safe places to live because they have guards or other security features. Others live on a compound because they enjoy the facilities and the presence of other foreigners. People are especially likely to feel this way if the culture in their host country is very different. To them living on a compound is like living in a safe retreat.

How do I communicate?

Whichever way works! One of the best things about living on a compound is that you get to meet people of different nationalities. This also can be a little confusing. It can be hard to communicate. You can start by finding out if you speak any of the same languages. You can also ask someone else to translate. If all else fails, you can always use signs and gestures.

> **REAL LIFE TIP**
> To meet your neighbors and make some new friends, take part in the neighborhood activities. You also can organize an event yourself. Neighborhood picnics or yard sales with the proceeds going to a local charity are a great way to meet friends.

Jumping Into New Hobbies and Interests

When living abroad, you learn many things. You learn about other cultures and traditions. You also may learn new and interesting hobbies. People in other countries might have hobbies that are not widely practiced in your own country. This is your opportunity to try a different sport, a new type of craft or musical instrument. Once you try it, you might like it so much that it becomes your new hobby. At first you might not be very good at it. However, the more you practice, the better you will get.

Name: Thai-Son
Age: 11
From: Vietnam
Lives in: Austria

"I go to the Vienna International School where I have learned to do lots of things. I've learned to play the recorder and the guitar. I started learning how to play the recorder when I was in third grade. I also have guitar lessons every week.

Since I moved abroad, I have learned several new hobbies. My favorite new hobby is roller-skating. In Austria lots of people roller-skate. I wanted to try it too. At first, I practiced by standing on the skates. I tried to keep my balance. After that, I started skating inside the house. I only went with minimum speed and tried to control the direction I was going.

Once I got used to skating inside the house, I tried skating in the playground. The ground was very soft. I also tried skating on the road and almost fell. I now skate normally, but still need to work on stopping. Every time I go skating, it's like being pounded in the leg by a ball.

I like to go skating in the spring, the summer, and the fall. This is when the ground is not too bumpy or slippery. Skating is my favorite hobby. I also take ice-skating lessons in school. Ice-skating is easy, because I already know how to skate. When I roller-skate I get lots of fresh air. Roller-skating is good for my health and I find it very interesting."

Name: Zacherie
Age: 11
From: France
Lives in: Indonesia
Used to live in: Burma and Sudan

"I have two hobbies. They are snorkeling and scuba diving. To go snorkeling you need a snorkel, a mask, and fins. When snorkeling, you swim and look underneath the water. To go scuba diving you need air in a tank. When scuba diving, you stay underwater and go deeper for a longer time.

I once went to the Red Sea with my parents and my family. We were on a boat for three days. I went snorkeling in different sites and saw lots of fish and corals. A man called Tim was on the boat with us. He went fishing and caught a coral grouper and a barracuda.

When I wasn't snorkeling, I played with my brother. We jumped off the boat into the water. It was very warm and clear. We had so much fun. We went to the Red Sea a second time. That time we went for five days. It was still fun, but I didn't snorkel as much. There was too much of a current.

A couple of years later, we moved to Indonesia. There we went to an island called Bunaken Island. The island was off another island called Sulawesi Island. I went snorkeling with a guide. His name was Jerry. It was very nice. I got chased by a triggerfish. They are black and yellow with white dots. They also have a beak like a parrotfish.

I went to Bunaken Island a second time. That time I went for my Padi Open Water Course. I went down at different levels. The deepest I went was 18 meters. I went to different places and sites to do exercises. Some of them were hard, but most of them were easy. I got to see sharks, turtles, moray eels, and cleaning shrimps. I also saw lots of colorful fish and coral. If I pass a test, I will be an official diver."

Name: Seth
Age: 11
From: United States
Lives in: Germany
Used to live in: Belgium

"One day at school my friend Daniel asked me to play soccer. Daniel was from England where people really like soccer. Daniel convinced me to play against the second graders. We were first graders and really wanted to beat the second graders. We worked harder and harder. I scored my first goal in one of the matches against the second graders. It was from the halfway line. When I was six, I was good enough to play for a club. Our coach was nice. His name was Danny. We were not very good, but we had fun.

I became the team's goalie, because I was tall, brave, and fought for the ball. I also became the goalie because I wanted to play that position. We didn't win any games. We usually tied or lost, but we still had fun. One time I was in a penalty shootout. The strongest shooter shot the ball. It went straight into my stomach. After that I was scared of the ball and became an even worse goalie.

Later I moved to Germany and started to play for another team. I made many friends and became a good soccer player. I improved partly because of my coach. Herr Schatz was very disciplined and strict. We were the champions for three years. After two years I started playing midfield. Some time later I changed schools and had to join a new team. Right now I play for the team in the village where I live. I have been playing striker or midfield.

This week I will play my first game with my new team. I am very excited to have my own jersey number and position. I hope to be a great soccer player when I grow up. I'm really good at soccer now and will never forget my German trainers."

Jumping Into New Hobbies and Interests Q&A

How do I know if I will like it?
You don't. You usually can not determine in advance whether you will like something. The best way to find out if you do is to try it. When living in another country, you might get the chance to try new things. It is a good idea to try lots of different things. Not only are you sure to have some unforgettable experiences, but you might even discover a new hobby.

Will I ever be able to learn this?
Yes! Learning something new is challenging. It takes a lot of practice to excel at something. You can train by yourself or in a group. You can also take lessons. At first getting the hang of your new hobby can seem daunting. You might even wonder if you will ever be able to get it right. Try, however, not to give up. The more you practice, the better you will get. Before you know it, you will have the skills required to perform your new hobby like a pro.

Would others want to do this too?
Maybe. Discovering a new hobby is rewarding. You want to practice it all the time. You might even want to share your passion with the world. You can

introduce others to your hobby by holding a presentation at school. You also might want to take a friend along next time you go. Once others know about your hobby, let them make up their own minds. After all just because you like it does not mean everyone else does.

REAL LIFE TIP
Be a mentor to others. Spending time coaching others is a great way to pass on your knowledge. Not only does the other person gain from your experience, but it helps you realize how far you have come.

Hospitable Hosting of Relatives and Other Guests

Finding out that your relatives are coming for a visit is always exciting. You can hardly wait to see them again. Once they arrive, everyone may feel a little overwhelmed. After all, you do not get to see each other every day. Sometimes it takes a little while to get used to each other. Other times, you may feel like you saw them yesterday. Because your family members have traveled a long way, they tend to stay for a while. This means that you have to share your space. It also means that you get to spend lots of time together. Spending time together allows you to catch up and to enjoy each other's company.

Name: Meredith
Age: 10
From: United States
Lives in: Germany

"I love it when people come to visit. Who wouldn't? I want them to see where and how I live. I also want to spend a lot of time with them. Most people that come to visit are relatives like my grandparents. Though my friends try to come, it's harder for them because of school schedules.

When people come to visit, it means that I get to hang out with them. I find out what's going on with them. I also get to tell them what's going on with me. One problem I have with writing and phoning people is that I am hesitant to tell them about my travels. I am afraid that they will think that I'm bragging. When people come to visit, I get to show them and that's not bragging.

When we have guests, we usually get to travel somewhere. My favorite places to visit are not all that touristy. I like going to the countryside in Italy or France. These places allow us time to relax instead of always being on the go. Then again, being on the go is good too.

I like going to Rome. It's a very busy place and there's a lot to see. The historical places are really interesting. We have to hurry if we want our guests to see everything. If we don't have time to travel with our family and friends, we just hang out. I like showing them my favorite places. I show them the local swimming pool and my favorite place in the park.

I also ask our visitors what they would like to see or do that day. Sometimes I tell them what I would normally do. My family and friends are often curious about what I do when they are not there. I show them as much as I can, but I try not to overdo it. After our visitors leave, I miss them a lot. I try not to focus on it. I try to think about how much fun the visit was. I also look forward to the next time we see each other."

Name: Jake
Age: 9
From: United States
Lives in: Kenya

"I live in Kisumu, which is a city in Kenya. I've lived here for one year. It's really hot in Kenya because we live right on the equator. There are a lot of cool animals. One animal I see a lot is the gecko. There are a lot of geckos around our house. Sometimes there are even geckos inside the house.

When my grandparents and aunt came to visit it was really fun. It's hard for them to visit me because I live on a different continent. When they were here we went to the Maasai Mara, which is a game reserve. The Maasai are warrior people. When we got to the reserve, we crossed a bridge. When we looked over the bridge, we saw hippos. Every day we went in our car or a game drive vehicle to look for animals. We saw a lot of cool animals like lions, hippos, crocodiles, warthogs, hyenas, wildebeest, zebras, gazelle, and elephants.

When my grandparents and my aunt saw all those animals they said it was the best vacation they had in their entire life. I liked having my relatives visit. It was fun and nice. No matter where I live, I enjoy it when my grandpa plays games with me and my grandma tells me stories. What made their visit extra special was that we did something that we never got to do with them before - see cool animals!"

Name: Rachelle
Age: 11
From: United States
Lives in: Taiwan

"I loved having Aunt Sandy over for a visit. The first day she was here, we got up early and visited with her. We were so excited to see her. I also loved having friends from the church back home come visit us even though they weren't relatives. We all went on a trip around the entire island. My brother Nathaniel and I rode our bikes to get breakfast for everybody.

While my aunt was here, we were like tourists. First, we went to see documentaries about Taiwan. I even learned some things and I've lived here for almost seven years. We went to the Chiang Kai Shek Memorial Hall. We looked at all the things that our tour guide showed us. We got to see the changing of the guards.

After lunch we left on our trip around the island. The first night we stayed in a cool aboriginal village. The people danced and sang. The hotel had little huts that were very fancy and comfortable. I loved it. We had a week of traveling to places I'd never been to and some we had seen before. It was really fun and I will never forget it. While we were on the trip, I celebrated my birthday. It was my best birthday ever."

Hospitable Hosting of Relatives and Other Guests Q&A

What should I show them?
Both the ordinary and the extraordinary. When people visit, you have chance to show off your new country. Take some time to tour the sites that make the area special. Show your guests some every day places as well. To you these places might not be anything special. Your guests, however, will be very interested in seeing where you go every day. Take them on a tour of your school or show them the playground in the park.

I don't feel like sharing my space. Now what?
Do it anyway! Though it's always fun to see your relatives, it can be a little

busy. You have to share your house and maybe even your bedroom. You are surrounded by people 24/7. You even have people around you when you feel like being alone. Try to be nice even when you do not feel like it. Your relatives are only here for a little while. Before you know it things will be back to normal. Your guests will be gone and the house will be yours again. Meanwhile enjoy spending time with your relatives. Once they leave, it will be some time before you see them again.

Why is it hard to say goodbye?

Because you know you are going to miss them. Saying goodbye at the end of a visit can be sad. Spending time together reminds you of how much you miss your relatives. What makes it even harder is that it might be a while before you see each other again. It is also hard because it is a case of everything or nothing. Either you see them all day long or not at all. Instead of focusing on how much you are going to miss them, remember all the fun times you shared. Do not forget that you can always call, write, or send an e-mail.

REAL LIFE TIP
Ask your relatives to bring some of your favorite foods from back home. As a thank you give them something from your host country. A local craft or special candy makes a great gift.

Family Vacations in Your Host Country

A great way to explore your host country is to go on vacation. Each time you go somewhere new, you discover more beautiful and fun places to visit. There is always something else to discover. Going on vacation usually means going farther than on a regular day trip. This allows you to see even more of your host country. You might go to the mountains, the ocean, or the desert. You might even discover places so special that you will want to share them with your family and friends next time they visit.

Name: Rosemary
Age: 10
From: Canada
Lives in: China

"During our first year in China, we visited the tropical island of Sanya. Sanya is sometimes referred to as 'China's Hawaii'. The climates on both islands are similar. We stayed near lots of beaches with lovely warm water and white sand. We went swimming at least once a day.

At one beach, there was a bad undertow. Because I was only five at the time, I was pulled underwater. It was traumatic. It was scary to be tumbling in the water. I didn't know which way was up and which way was down. It was especially hard because I couldn't swim. It happened to me twice.

We ate lots of great food, including seafood. We also tried a delicious vegetable called *four-corner-beans*. They were a type of bean plant. They were delicious fried with garlic. We also tried a type of fruit that comes from a cactus. It was called *prickly pear*. It tasted like raspberries. We also had seafood, including prawns, scallop-like shellfish, and ocean fish.

There were lots of beautiful shells on the beaches. We collected one or two large bags full of shells. We took them back with us. We collected lots of different shells. For the most part, we collected the shells that we called 'unicorn horns'. They were small twisted shells, which were fat at the opening and gradually thin off to a point. They were inhabited by crab-like creatures, so we had to be careful.

We also bought some shells. They were beautiful, smooth, and iridescent. Looking back on it, I feel a bit guilty. We probably shouldn't have bought the shells. After all the animals inside were probably boiled and eaten. We were also given some pieces of coral.

Mom and dad were happy that my sister and I could help translate for them because we had been attending Chinese school. We didn't translate everything. Sometimes we'd just go into the restaurant's kitchen and point to what we wanted to eat. The cook would make it for us. Eventually it was time to return home. We had to go back to school, but it was fun while we were there."

Name: Julia
Age: 8
From: United States
Lives in: Germany

"My family and I like to go to the Mosel region of Germany. One time we stayed in a hotel in the mountains. The hotel had a swimming pool. We went for a walk and found a nice green meadow with some goats and a donkey. We fed the goats and tried to feed the donkey. The donkey wasn't interested. He took one look at us and started eating again.

My favorite goat was a gray baby goat. He really liked me when I fed him. The goats kept butting each other out of the way. They all wanted to get close to the sweet, fresh grass we were feeding them. I forgot to mention the geese. They were greedy little beggars because they took almost all the food.

We went swimming every single day we were there. When we were in Germany, we went to a castle on top of a mountain. There was a man with a dog and three ferrets. The dog kept barking, but the ferrets were very nice. The man let us pet the ferrets.

My favorite food in Germany is *weinerschitzel*. It's a thin piece of pork. It can come with all kinds of sauces. My favorite sauce is the mushroom sauce. It is divine! I also like German ice cream. They have chocolate, vanilla, strawberry, gummy bear, and many other flavors. They also have vanilla, chocolate, and strawberry mixed. I like going on holiday in Germany. I especially like the delicious food and the nice places to see."

Name: Angelina
Age: 9
From: United States
Lives in: Mexico
Has also lived in: Ecuador

"It's fun to live overseas. I've been to lots of places. I've been to the Amazon Rain Forest, the Galapagos Islands, Ecuador, and Peru. In the Amazon Rain Forest, I went into a beautiful forest where I saw lots of pretty and colorful birds. I also saw pink river dolphins and some translucent butterflies. We rode in canoes on the river and hiked through the forest. I even cut my hand on a machete. It hurt! I also saw lots of trees. The natives communicate by hitting the sides of trees with their machetes.

When we went to the Galapagos Islands, we lived on a boat for a week. We saw sea lions, iguanas, and more pretty birds. I wanted to touch the sea lions, but my mom told me not to. She said that we're not supposed to bother them. We also went snorkeling. When we looked we saw that we were surrounded by sea lions. Then a wave pushed my big brother into the sea lions. We didn't know who was more surprised: the sea lions or my brother. It was really cool.

When we lived in Ecuador, I went to Peru during spring break. We went on a small plane to fly over the Nazca lines, which are huge carvings in the ground. I got airsick on the plane. We also went to a museum with really neat preserved bodies. Some of them had hair that went beyond their feet. We also went to Machu Pichu, which are ruins up in the mountains. We took a train to get there. It was Carnival and one of the traditions is throwing water balloons. We had our window open and a kid through a water balloon through our window as the train passed. It hit me and my mom.

There were lots of ruins in Machu Pichu and we had to climb a lot to get there. I liked seeing the llamas. I even got to hold a baby llama. Living overseas is the best thing that ever happened to me!"

Family Vacations in Your Host Country Q&A

Should I prepare?

Yes! Getting ready to go on a trip is almost as much fun as actually going. Planning all the adventures you are going to have can put a smile on your face. To best know what to expect, find out a few things about where you are going. It also helps you decide where to go when you get there and what to bring. A great way to learn more about your destination is to surf the Internet. Besides practical information, you will be able to see pictures of your destination.

What is the big deal?

A vacation in your host country might not sound extraordinary. After all, a vacation is nothing more than a few fun-filled days away. However, exploring your new country is a unique opportunity. While it is hard to imagine, you will probably not live in your host country forever. Try to enjoy everything that makes living in this part of the world special. Have lots of fun and see lots of sights. That way you will have wonderful memories.

How can I help?

Sometimes on vacation, you see people or animals that need help. You may encounter homeless and hungry people or sick animals and feel sad. You might even come across a natural area that could use some help. Talk to your parents about what you can do as a family. Maybe you can raise money for a charity or volunteer your time. You also can help out through education and learning more about issues. Once you have more information, you might be able to contribute in other ways.

REAL LIFE TIP
Before your vacation, save your allowance for a few weeks to buy a souvenir. A little memento from your vacation is sure to become a treasured object.

PART FIVE

THE REALITIES

Homesick at Home

When you are homesick, you miss the place that you used to live a lot. You miss it so much that it hurts. Homesickness makes you feel sad. It can also make you feel lonely, confused, and even angry. Most children who live abroad get homesick occasionally. When you get homesick, it does not always mean that you do not like your host country. In fact, you actually can feel homesick when doing something fun. Imagine, for example, that it is your birthday. Even though you are having fun, you might suddenly miss your best friend who used to come to all your parties.

Name: David
Age: 7
From: Argentina and the United States
Lives in: Romania
Used to live in: Venezuela

"I've been in Romania for four months and still get homesick sometimes. My friends in Venezuela were a lot of fun. When I left they threw me a big party. They also gave me presents so I wouldn't forget them. My favorite present was the white teddy bear that they all signed.

When I first got here, I really missed my home in Venezuela. I would cry in the car on the way home every afternoon. I didn't feel like I was really going home. I started to feel better when our shipment arrived. Suddenly there were more familiar things in our apartment.

Even after school started I still missed my friends a lot. I'm glad that they still send me e-mails and pictures. I called my friend Benjamin once. I also e-mailed my teacher Ms. Lauren and told her how I was doing. I still miss my friends and my old school.

When I get homesick, I ask my mom why we had to come to Romania. I also ask her why we couldn't have stayed in Venezuela. I feel better when I talk to my mom. She gives me hugs and reminds me of why she needed the job in Romania.

I started to feel better when I got a puppy. My mom had promised me one a long time ago, but we couldn't have one in our old apartment. Now I get to play with my puppy when I get home. I also feel better when I have play dates or sleepovers with my new friends in Bucharest."

Name: Kara
Age: 11
From: United States
Lives in: Indonesia

"Most people think that I get homesick while I'm in Indonesia, but I don't. I get homesick when I go back to the United States. I love it here in Indonesia and really don't like to leave. My home is here in Indonesia. I've lived here almost my whole life.

When I go to the United States for a visit, I get really homesick. We spend a lot of time traveling because we have to visit lots of people. It's very hard for me because we're in a different place almost every night. The only good thing is that I don't have much time to think about my homesickness.

When I'm in the United States, I miss tons of things about Indonesia. I miss being able to sit on my porch and feel the breeze. I also miss hearing every sort of bird I never thought existed. These birds are here year round because there are no seasons that force them to migrate. Indonesia is gorgeous. There are no forest reserves even though almost the whole island is beautiful jungle.

Most people, unless they live here, might think that I'm crazy for liking it here. However it's not all jungle. There are beautiful beaches with great sand and not many people. The water is an absolutely lovely color and has the perfect temperature. I love going to the beach here. I think it's wonderful to live here and find it really hard to leave. I love it. Some people might not want to live on an island where not many people go, but I do!"

Name: Ben
Age: 12
From: United States
Lives in: Laos
Used to live in: Vietnam

"I miss quite a few things from the United States. I especially miss some of my favorite foods. Luckily my grandmothers send me things such as noodles and cheddar cheese goldfish crackers. We usually buy food and school supplies in Thailand. It's only about 24 kilometers to the border. It can be hard to find things where we live. Things also tend to be expensive. I miss being able to buy things easily.

When my brother and I have our birthdays, our parents allow us to order something through the Internet. My dad says that sometimes it seems like our lives revolve around shopping on the Internet. I've been disappointed a few times with items that didn't work right because of the voltage differences. When that happens it makes me a little homesick. I get over it quickly because I remind myself that people in Laos are very poor and that kids my age have very few games or toys.

When I get homesick, it's usually in a dream that projects my view of a perfect life with everything that I could ever ask for. When I wake up I look at a memory from the United States. This makes me realize that the dream was just that – a dream. To make myself feel better, I think about all the things I did back home and can still do here. Sometimes I can do them even better here. For example, I can ride my bicycle better because there's not much traffic. I also get to go on some pretty wild trips like to the dark caves of Vang Vieng or Luang Prabang. Some of our friends back home assume that kids living overseas are always homesick. It's not like that. Living overseas is just a different experience than living at home. In my opinion, kids living abroad are just like other kids. Just because we move around the world doesn't mean that we're much different from our friends back home. Living overseas just gives us a different way of looking at things."

Homesick at Home Q&A

Why do I feel this way?

Because when you move abroad, you leave behind many things. You miss the secure feeling and familiarity of the people and the places that mean a lot to you. It is because these things are important to you that you miss them from time to time. Homesickness is just a reminder that you are missing something. You could think of it as a blessing. It is because you love these things that you miss them so much.

Will I ever feel better?

Yes! Nobody likes feeling homesick. After all, missing something or somebody feels awful. When it comes to homesickness, there are no rules. Every situation and every person is different. Some people feel sad for only a few minutes. Others feel sad for as long as a few days. There is, however, one thing for sure. It does pass! Until then remind yourself that these feelings are only temporary. Before you know it, you will feel better.

What can I do?

Lots of things! You can talk to someone and tell them how you feel. Sharing your feelings makes you feel lighter because your feelings are no longer bottled up inside. If you miss a person, you can write that person a letter or an e-mail. You might even be able to call them. You also can distract yourself by doing something fun. Try to involve someone else. Together you can go for a walk, play a game, or work on a project.

REAL LIFE TIP
When you miss another country you used to live in, hold a special family night. Ask your parents to cook a national dish. Look at old photographs and talk about when you used to live there. Reminiscing can be almost as good as actually being there!

Happy Birthday to ME!!

Cake, candles, streamers, balloons and presents most likely are among the "must haves" of your birthday party tradition. Once you live abroad, everything is different and this includes the way you celebrate your special day. Celebrating your birthday abroad can be extra fun. It also can seem a little crazy, especially if you have just moved to your host country. Don't let that stop you from having a wonderful day. So whether its Eid milaad saeed, Joyeuz Anniversaire or Alles Gute Zom Gebrutstage, remember your birthday only comes once a year.

Name: Olivia
Age: 8
From: United States
Lives in: France

"I moved to France when I was six years old. I celebrated my seventh birthday three months after we moved. I wasn't sure how I was going to celebrate it. I had only just begun to learn the language and was still making friends. My mother also had trouble doing all the things she did back home. She was busy setting up our new home and didn't have much time to learn the language. We didn't know where to get invitations, decorations, or party favors.

We decided on a day and invited many of my friends from school. We didn't know their addresses and had trouble talking to them on the phone. Luckily we figured it out. My friends at the party came from many different countries. They came from Japan, Sweden, England, Holland, Denmark and other countries.

After the party my mom said that it was a very quiet celebration. This was because we didn't have a common language yet. All of us were just beginning to learn French and many of the girls didn't understand English very well. We used gestures to communicate. We played games, decorated crowns with jewels and played on a big, bouncy, jumpy gym that my parents rented for the party.

My best gift was a little kitten. She was for the whole family and we named her Mia. I also got a cake from my teacher. It was delicious because it tasted a lot like the cakes back home.

This year my party was easier to organize and louder. I had a Lizzie McGuire party. We shopped for birthday supplies when we went home this summer. We saved glass yogurt jars and my friends and I painted them with special paint to make candles for our rooms. My mom went to a copy store and had journals made out of different pieces of colored paper. All my friends decorated these with stickers.

The party room was decorated with streamers and balloons. I even had a *Joyeux Anniversaire* banner. We watched a Lizzie McGuire movie and sang karaoke to her latest CD. The best part was a firecracker that we put on the cake while everyone sang happy birthday. My birthdays have been fantastic. I'll never forget turning seven and eight years old in France."

Name: Zandre
Age: 11
From: South Africa
Lives in: Turkey
Used to live in: Egypt

"I've just celebrated my eleventh birthday. It's my second birthday in Turkey. It was very different than the ones I had in Pretoria. In South Africa my birthdays were in the summer. In Turkey my birthdays are in the winter. In Turkey there's not much to do. School ends at 3 p.m. and birthday parties are on the weekend. In South Africa, I could have a birthday party during the week.

Back in South Africa, I usually had a party at a steak house. We would play games, eat hamburgers, and hang out. For my ninth birthday we went to a water park and enjoyed the day there. It was so fun. We swam in the wave pool and went down the shoots.

In Turkey most parties are either at home or at the bowling alley or cinema. For my last party we showed a DVD, played ten-pin bowling, and had hamburgers at the sports club. It snowed and rained. My mom ordered a cake from a *patisserie*. I invited the whole class. There are only nine students. My friends are from different countries. My two best friends are Turkish.

I still miss my old school friends from South Africa. I would like them to be at my parties. I still go and see them when we go home on leave. Unfortunately they have changed and we now like different things. I also miss my grandparents coming to my parties. I usually get a card in the mail and a gift when I see them eight months later. Sometimes they ask my mom to buy a gift from them, but it's not the same."

Name: Melissa
Age: 12
From: United States
Used to live in: Swaziland, Japan, and South Africa

"Ever imagine moving on your birthday? How about moving to a different continent on your birthday? That is part of living overseas, especially when your birthday is in the summer month of August. Many kids are cursed with this situation and I am one of them. Out of the twelve birthdays I've had, I've only formally celebrated eight. One reason I don't like moving on my birthday is because we are so busy packing or unpacking that we have no time for a party. Many times we have to throw something together. For instance, on my 8th birthday in Japan we only went to an ice cream store with some neighbors. Once we got to our new house, we didn't know anyone to invite.

There are ways of making your birthday better. For instance, when you are back home you can use your experiences from living abroad to make an international theme party. Also when you are living abroad, you can invite a variety of people. That's what we did for my 12th birthday in South Africa. I invited friends from church, school, and the embassy. We had a mini Olympics party and each guest represented their country. Everyone enjoys meeting new people. If you only have a few friends, ask them to bring a friend or two. Thinking of a theme that will intrigue your guests will help. If you are having fun, there is a 75% chance that your friends are having fun too. Sometimes they like the party even more than you do.

I can only hope that these wise words will help. After all, everyone's overseas adventures are different. I usually stay for two to three years at a post, while others stay longer or shorter. But one thing to always remember is that even if you can't have a party every year, someone, somewhere, is wishing you happiness on your special day."

Happy Birthday to ME!! Q&A

Why isn't it the same?

Because in your host country everything is different, including the way you celebrate your birthday. Your relatives will likely not be able to attend your party and most of your gifts will be packages in the mail. The weather, food and the party favors also might be different. Yet no matter how many differences, one thing stays the same. Your birthday is your special day. Celebrate!!!

What if don't have anyone to invite?

It takes a while to make new friends. The first time you celebrate your birthday abroad, you might not know who to invite. You do not know the other children at school well enough. And you have not played with the other children in the neighborhood yet. However, having a party is the perfect way to get to know the other children. Invite those children who seem friendly and have some fun. After all, everyone likes a good party.

How can I make it fun?

By doing something special. Instead of having a typical party, be creative. Do something you have always wanted to try. Maybe you can horseback ride or scuba dive. Bring along a friend, sister, brother, or your entire family. Nothing is more fun than sharing a special experience with others. Do not forget to bring along a camera to capture your special day.

REAL LIFE TIP
Save your gifts for your birthday! Presents sent by mail sometimes arrive early. It is tempting to open them before your special day. Don't! Saving them until your birthday is much more rewarding. And besides trying to guess what is inside is half the fun.

Pen Pals, Blogs and Text Messages. Staying in Touch

When you live abroad, you will want to stay in touch with your loved ones back home and your friends who have moved on to different places. You might even have brothers or sisters who live elsewhere. Staying in touch is a lot of work, yet very rewarding. Luckily technology has made it easier to stay in touch. It used to take many weeks before a letter reached its destination. Now you can connect instantly through e-mail or by phone.

Name: Natalie
Age: 13
From: United States
Lives in: France

"When I moved to France, I had just turned ten years old. I missed all the friends and family I had left behind in the United States. I knew that I would really have to make an effort to stay in touch with them. I have my own room. I also have a new desk and my very own computer. This way I look forward to writing them even more.

Mostly I use e-mail to communicate with them. I think that it's amazing that a message can travel across continents in a matter of minutes. I can type faster than I can write, so the message gets written faster. Sometimes I have problems with the whole electronic thing. When that happens I send letters. I like writing letters because I can use cute stationary and personalize it a little more.

About every month I call my family and friends or they call me. Sometimes I can express myself better on the phone than in writing. My grandfather was just diagnosed with a terrible disease and it's good to hear his voice. I just have to remember that there is a big time difference. I am eight hours ahead from friends in Wyoming and seven hours ahead from relatives in Texas.

Staying in touch is very important to me because we support each other to cure homesickness. My friends also encourage me in basically everything I do. They are anxious to hear about what's going on here and I'm always interested in what's happening there. I always like receiving news from them.

If I want to keep receiving news, I have to do my part to reciprocate. I always look forward to receiving letters and information from them, and they probably enjoy it from me. Without the support from my friends this move would have been much harder for my family and me. That's why I try to do my part by staying in touch and most of my good friends also do their part. It's really a cycle from me to them."

Name: Fiona
Age: 12
From: United States
Lives: Botswana

"Laura was an amazing friend. We spent one and a half years together and became best friends. Then I had to move and here I am in Botswana. I always expected Laura would remember her promise to e-mail me every day. It turns out she didn't. I expected daily updates about what was going on at my old school. Did Anthony say something funny? Did Cara write something amazing and rip it up? And what about Laura herself? How were things with her family?

I thought Laura and I would be friends for a long time. I thought that she would be waiting for me when I came back for a visit. I guess that didn't happen though. I've received lots of forwarded e-mails, but only a handful of e-mails written by Laura. A while ago, it started to bug me. I wrote her to ask why she could send me thousands of forwards, but not a simple sentence about how she is doing. She never answered that e-mail either.

I let it go for a while. Then my dad installed a phone where I can call much cheaper. I got excited and called Laura. She barely said anything and ended that she had to go eat. I slipped her my number and then she hung up. I waited a while for her to call me back but it hasn't happened. It would be easy for her to dial that number but she hasn't. I was devastated at her brisk good-bye. Now I am devastated that she hasn't called me still.

I told my friend Garrett that I feel replaced. I also told him that I miss everyone so much. He said that they don't have replacements for me just backups. He also said that I was not coming back for a while and that they have to find new friends too. Garrett was never great with words but these words meant a lot. It made me think that maybe Laura was not such a bad friend after all. Staying in touch is hard and I lost a friend. All I can say to Laura is "Thank you. You were a great friend."

Name: Erin
Age: 12
From: United States
Lives in: China
Has also lived in: Hong Kong and Kuala Lumpur

"When I was 1 1/2 years old, I moved to Hong Kong with my family. At that time my family included my parents, my twin brother, my brother, and my sister. We moved again when I was 3. This time we moved to Kuala Lumpur. We were all together for about 2 1/2 years. Then my brother John graduated from high school and left for college.

I felt lonely because I missed my brother and my sister was busy with her high school friends. We moved again to Beijing shortly after John left. I was excited about the move, but still missed my brother. I called John every week and I loved talking to him. Then my sister Meghan graduated from high school and went to the United States to go to college as well. That was really difficult for me because I was really close to Meghan. We talk on the phone at least once a week and we e-mail each other a lot.

I do feel lucky because John and Meghan come to visit us at Christmas. We also get to see them in the summer when we go home for a long vacation. However, last summer was disappointing because Meghan was working at a camp that wasn't close by. I was only able to see her a few times over the whole summer. Because I hardly saw her, I make more of an effort to stay in touch.

The hardest part about living abroad is being away from my brother and sister. I miss them."

Pen Pals, Blogs and Text Messages. Staying in Touch Q&A

Why should I stay in touch?

Because it's worth it! Staying in touch can be a lot of work. It takes time to write a letter or an e-mail. It also takes brainpower to come up with things to write. However, friends and family are one of the most important things in life. Let others know that you have not forgotten them. And while it may be hard to stay in touch, the effort is well worth it. Hearing from a loved-one is exciting. It is also good to know that people care about you.

How can I stay in touch?

There are many ways to stay in touch. You can use instant messaging, send e-mails or write letters. Instant messaging allows you to have a real time conversation, even if it is a quick "Hi!". This might be a challenge if you are living in different time zones. The good thing about e-mail is that your message reaches the person fast. Another good thing is that many people type faster than they write. A downside of e-mail is that not everyone has regular access to the Internet, particularly if you are living in a developing country. If that is the case, you can always write a letter. You might even be able to call your friends. Calling long distance may be expensive though, so talk with your parents before making that call.

What if we grow apart?

People change and so do friendships. Sometimes you grow in the same direction. Other times you grow in a different direction. It's sad to realize you and your friend no longer share as much in common. Once upon a time you could finish each other's sentences. Now you hardly know what to say to each other any more. Don't give up on your friendship too quickly. Even though you might be into different things, it doesn't mean you no longer care for each other as friends.

REAL LIFE TIP
If you have a digital camera, use it! Digital cameras are a great way to send pictures by e-mail. With your parents' permission, you might even consider putting up your own website or starting a blog. That way you can post pictures and stories about all your experiences.

Sick Days

Getting sick is always a drag!! Getting sick while living abroad can be even worse. Besides not feeling well, you might be a little scared. It can be especially scary if you don't know what's wrong with you. Luckily, a visit to the doctor usually clears things up. Doctors all over the world are trained to diagnose and treat patients. After an examination and perhaps some tests, your doctor will be able to tell what is wrong with you. Before you know it, you will be on the road to recovery.

Name: Christian
Age: 11
From: United States
Lives in: Indonesia

"I've been sick twice. The first time I got sick I was in the second grade. I got really bad malaria. It felt like someone put a lead block on my back. When my mom took my temperature it went up to 104 degrees Fahrenheit. Once we got to the clinic they took a blood test. Then they gave me some medication and I got better.

I got malaria by being bitten by an infected female mosquito. When I got malaria I didn't feel sick until a week or two later. My symptoms included fever, chills, and vomiting. Some treatments for malaria are unusual. Some people cut themselves to get the "bad blood" out. Others drink papaya leaf tea to prevent malaria. I hear this is really gross.

People in Indonesia also have unusual treatments for other things. When someone gets a cold they rub a coin on their chest to cure it. The second time I got sick, I had an infection in my appendix. It hurt so much. When I slept, it felt like I was sleeping on a sharp rock. In the morning I went to the clinic and they gave me medication.

My siblings came in. They made me laugh which hurt. Then the doctor came. He told me I might need surgery. They flew me to Timika. During the flight I passed out. Once I got to the hospital it turned out that I didn't need surgery. All I needed was some medicine. After three or four days I went home."

Name: Kenna
Age: 6
From: United States
Lives in: Austria

"One time I got sick in Vienna. I went to the Wilhelmina Hospital. I needed more liquids in my body and had to stay in the hospital. I felt sad because I couldn't be with my sister or go to school. I felt weak and sick and the needle in my arm hurt. The hospital smelled funny, like rubber. I was scared of being really sick. I was also scared of the doctors. They spoke German and I wished they would speak English. I didn't know much German yet.

Then the hospital had a nice idea. They had doctors dressed like clowns. The clowns came to my room. They thought my stuffed unicorn was a different kind of animal. They called it a donkey and a giraffe. When they found out that my German wasn't very good, they spoke English. They wore red noses. One clown was a boy and one was a girl.

I think this is a nice program because it helped me feel a little better. After the visit from the clowns, I got to go home the very next day. My house smelled great. I was glad to be home. Later I found out that the clown program is a special program. It is called *Rote Nase*. The clowns help sick kids smile in the hospital.

My mom has a *Rote Nase* T-shirt. It has a red nose on it and says '*Heute Schon gelacht?*' It means 'Have you laughed today yet?' My mom bought it to help the clown program because she liked how they helped me. I'm glad the clown doctors helped me smile for a while and forget that I was sick."

Name: Adam
Age: 7
From: United States
Lives in: Kenya

"Once I got hurt here. I was in the shower and my dad knocked on the door to tell me to get out. The shower door was made of glass and it broke. I guess it wasn't the right kind of glass for shower doors. We didn't know that until it was too late. A big piece of glass fell on my elbow and my knee because I was sitting down in the shower.

My dad was really sorry. My mom is a nurse and she came in. The cut on my elbow wasn't very big but the one on my knee was huge. It was about three inches long and one inch deep. It hurt a lot and I was scared. My mom called a few doctors and we all went to the hospital.

They put eight stitches in my knee and two in my elbow. It hurt badly while they were putting them in. I kept asking if we were done yet. Once the stitches were in, it didn't hurt very much. After a week they took the stitches out. I got a homemade crutch that I had to use for about six days. I couldn't run or jump on the trampoline for about two weeks but I can now.

My knee has a big scar. I think it's awesome because it looks like a snake that is shedding its skin. It doesn't hurt at all anymore. They made the new shower door shatterproof. I'm not scared of taking a shower anymore. The only thing that scares me is having a *matatu* run over me. *Matatus* are little buses that people get rides in. The drivers are crazy, but I am careful around traffic. I don't cross the road when I see one coming."

Sick Days Q&A

What can I get?
It depends on where you live. Different parts of the world pose different health risks. In a tropical country, you have to be careful not to get sunburned. In a cold climate, you have to protect yourself from frostbite. Find out what you can do to stay healthy by talking with your parents and your teachers. Staying healthy might be as simple as wearing sunscreen or gloves when you go out.

Should I be afraid?
No! Nonetheless, chances are that you will get sick at least once while living abroad. Abroad, like at home, you will likely catch the occasional bug. And while being sick is no fun, you should not worry. Just give it some time. After a few days of rest and relaxation, you will be back to your old self. The chance of you catching anything worse than a cold or the flu is slim. So relax and enjoy yourself.

Is there anything I can do?
Yes! There are plenty of things you can do to stay healthy. You can start by

taking care of your body. You can do this by eating nutritious food, drinking lots of water, and getting plenty of rest and exercise. You also should wash your hands with soap and wear clothes appropriate for the climate when you go outside. Doing these things might not always prevent illness, yet you will recover quicker if you are healthy.

REAL LIFE TIP
Laugh a lot! Not only does it make you happy, but it also keeps you healthy. When you laugh you raise the level of infection fighting cells. This in turn strengthens your immune system.

Visiting the Homeland

Even when you feel at home in your host country, a trip to the homeland can be a welcome change of scenery. There is nothing quite like being in your own country. You can speak your own language and eat the foods you missed. You can also spend time with your friends and family. While you were away some things might have changed. After all, things do not stand still just because you no longer live there. Other things might have stayed the same, but feel different. This is probably because living abroad has given you a new perspective.

Name: Joshua
Age: 10
From: United States
Lives in: Indonesia

"When I go back to the United States I don't feel in the right place. I get homesick. I've lived overseas so long that my home is in Indonesia. When I go to the States I have to pack and unpack all my things. Packing may take two or more weeks and unpacking takes even longer. When I unpack I only take the stuff I need out of the suitcase instead of dumping it all on the floor. This is why unpacking can take a very long time.

Another hard thing about going to the States is the jetlag. It makes my day twice as long. It's a weird feeling because I need to change my watch every time I go to a different place. The hardest thing about going to the States is making friends. It's hard because I'm different from everyone else. I'm different because I don't know everything they know and they don't know everything I know. I'm also different in the way I do things and the things I like.

I'm going to the States this summer. Thankfully, I'm only staying for six months! One fun thing about going is that I get to see all my cousins, aunts, uncles, and grandparents. I do like some things about going to the United States, but I like being in Indonesia more. I'd be happy to just stay home."

Name: Lili
Age: 9
From: Spain
Lives in: Malawi

"Arriving at the airport in Spain, I feel very excited. I wonder what color rental car we will get this time. I like red cars the best. Yes!! We get a huge, red, brand new, shiny car. Our car in Africa is about twenty years old and most things on it are broken. People are really friendly and speak to me in Spanish. It feels as though I'm home again. The main roads are all smooth. In Africa, the roads are full of holes and mud. I shout out the names of all the big shops and cinemas.

The door of our house is like a wooden castle gate. It's made of stone and the floor upstairs is solid wood. The downstairs floor is granite. It's nice and cool on my feet especially on a hot day. In Spain, I watch TV as I eat breakfast. In Malawi, I don't have a TV, only videos. I like the advertisements, because they are nearly all songs. There are lots of cartoons and in the evening I watch scary movies before I go out.

When I was new to the village, some girls asked if I wanted to play with them. We played tag with the boys in the plaza. Playing tag in Spain is different than playing tag in Malawi. The girls come to fetch me every night because I'm the youngest. In Malawi I go to bed at eight o'clock. In Spain I don't go out until ten o'clock at night when it's dark and there are lots of children screaming around the plaza.

I buy ice cream and bubble gum. One euro is enough to buy plenty of sweets. There are lots of *fiestas* with music in the plaza. Sometimes my old friends from Madrid visit me. We play upstairs with our toys, tell scary stories, and sleep in the attic. Last time when I went back to Malawi, lots of children came to say goodbye."

Name: Emilie
Age: 10
From: Norway
Used to live in: United States

"When I was living in the United States, I used to go back to Norway in the summer. It took a long time to fly back on the airplane. I visited my family, my friends, and my school friends. I also went to Bardufoss to see my family. That was a lot of fun. I also tasted Norwegian chocolate and candy. It was very good to sample the sweets again.

I went to this big swimming hall. There was a slide, a Jacuzzi, and a diving board. I was very excited. We also went shopping in Bardufoss and Trondheim. Bardufoss is a small place to shop. Trondheim is a bigger place to shop because it's a city. My mom was born in Bardufoss and my dad in Trondheim.

I also went to my grandparent's summer cabin. I liked it because we went fishing on land and in a boat. We also went fishing for crabs. My cousin and my sister and I made a house that we played in. The house had no roof.

Summer time in Norway can be rainy and cold, but I didn't care. Back in Houston it would be warm and sunny for a long time. Every time we went back to Norway, I used to visit my best friend Julie. We played with each other and with her brother. It was very exciting to see her after a long time. Julie has been my best friend since I was one year old. It was sad to say goodbye to all my friends and family until the next summer."

Visiting the Homeland Q&A

Why am I confused?
Because it takes time to adjust. Even though visiting the homeland is fun, it can also be confusing. As you drive by your old house, you realize that another family now lives there. You also realize that you are no longer a part of things the way you used to be. While other children still take the school bus to your old school, you no longer go there. Give yourself some time to adjust. Once you settle in, things will no longer seem so confusing.

What if I miss my things?
Most trips to the homeland are busy. However, even during the most fun-filled vacation, you may miss your own things. Suddenly you do not feel like going on another family outing. You may want to be in your own bed, in your own room, surrounded by your own things. Remind yourself that you will be home soon. Until then, spend time with your family and friends and visit some of your favorite sites. Most of all, enjoy yourself.

Can I feel at home in more than one place?

Yes! It is a very special feeling to feel at home somewhere. Feeling at home means feeling safe, comfortable, and connected. You feel that you are a part of the place and the place is a part of you. Just like you can love more than one person, you can be at home in more than one place. Many children who live abroad feel at home in both their host country and their home country. You do not have to choose between them. You can love them both!

REAL LIFE TIP
Bring back a supply of your favorite goodies. That way you are sure to satisfy your next craving once you return to your host country.

PART SIX

THE JOURNEY CONTINUES

Mentoring Other Kids

Remember when you first moved abroad? Everything was new and you had so much to learn. With the help of your new friends and classmates, you gradually started to feel more comfortable. After a while, things even began to make sense. One day, you felt at home. When new children arrive, you realize how far you have come. Now you have a chance to help out by showing other kids the way.

Name: Cindy
Age: 9
From: Australia and Thailand
Lives in: Vietnam
Used to live in: China, Indonesia, and Papua New Guinea

"On my first day of school my teacher introduced me to all the kids in my class. I didn't know who they were or what their names were. No one knew who I was. Luckily a lot of kids raised their hands to be my buddy and show me around the school. That's how I knew that a lot of people liked me.

At recess my buddy showed me around the school and told me about the games they play. The games were completely different than the games in my own country. Once the other students knew me better, they asked if I wanted to play a game with them. I started to feel like they really liked me.

My friends come from Korea, Japan, Germany, South Africa, and the United States. Some of them speak a different language. I understand them when they speak English to me. As soon as the kids got to know me, I was invited to sleepovers and birthday parties. That made me feel really good."

Name: Nicola
Age: 10
From: United States
Lives in: Austria

"When I first moved here, not many of the other kids helped me out. I didn't like figuring things out on my own, so I decided to help other kids who needed help. And that is exactly what I did. When I was in the second grade, a Danish girl named Theresa came to my school. She didn't speak English, so it was very hard for her. All of our classes are in English, except our German lessons. You can only start German lessons when you know English well enough.

I started helping Theresa the very first day of the second grade. Together with my friend Rachel, we taught Theresa basic English words. I pointed to objects and told her what they were called. For example, I would point to the swing and say the word 'swing' or I would point to rocks and say 'rocks'. We went on like that for a long time.

My teacher asked me to sit with Theresa so that I could help her with other things. I helped her by taking her to the nurse and by showing her where the bathrooms were. I also told her how to get lunch and what the class and school rules were.

Theresa took English as a Second Language classes and learned to speak English almost fluently. She knows so much of it that she can take German classes like me. Theresa also can read and write stories in English. She does very well on her spelling tests. Theresa and I have become good friends. We are now in fourth grade and have the same teacher. It makes me feel proud to see how much a little bit of extra help can pay off."

Name: Beatrice
Age: 9
From: United Kingdom
Lives in: Malawi
Used to live in: Belgium

"When I came to Malawi, I was very excited. I had only one worry and that was whether I was going to make any friends. I tried to imagine my new friends, but as soon as I saw them they were totally different. I was five when I came to Malawi and so I started in kindergarten.

In my school in Malawi, the first thing I tried to do was to remember everybody's name. The other children made me feel welcome. At break time, the first people I saw were Hafsa, Zainub, Natasha, and Kim. We used to sing nursery rhymes and play catch. The one name I kept forgetting was Natasha's name. The only thing I could remember was that it had a lot 'a's in it.

I was very lucky to have friends because I was always shy and quiet. As the years went by I started changing friends. By my third year, Natasha had become my best friend. Unfortunately she left for India in my fourth year. Now I have lots of friends and lots of sleepovers. I even go on safari with my friends. Sometimes I even go without my parents.

I went to Victoria Falls in Zimbabwe with one of my friends. We had a wonderful time together. Recently I went on a radio show with another friend. We talked about our favorite songs. I have made lots of friends in Malawi. I know that they might leave or I might leave. When that happens I have to start making new friends all over again."

Mentoring Other Kids Q&A

Why should I bother to help? Can't they figure things out on their own?
Helping others might sound like a big inconvenience. However, passing along your knowledge is rewarding and empowering. It was not so long ago that you were the new kid. Remember all the things you wished you had known when you first arrived and had to learn. Not only does it feel great to help someone out, but it also makes you realize how far you have come. Now you are the one giving the advice and you can feel proud.

Do they even want my help?
Yes! New children might appear withdrawn and shy. This might give you the impression that they do not want your help. Don't be fooled. Underneath the facade they are probably just scared. After all, they have just arrived in a new country and do not know what to expect. Don't wait for new children to come up to you. Take the initiative! Start with an introduction and tell them a little bit about yourself.

What can I do?
Lots of things! You can introduce yourself and offer to give the person a tour. You can also ask the person to sit with you at lunch and introduce them to your friends. You can even invite them to play with you at recess or ask you parents to invite them to dinner. Finally, you can show them the ropes and give them useful information.

> **REAL LIFE TIP**
> Invite new children to your next party. This makes them feel welcome and appreciated. It also allows them to meet some other children and have some fun. At the same time, you get the opportunity to make another friend.

Migrating Season: Saying Goodbye to Friends

When you first move abroad, you usually will not know anyone. After a while you make friends and begin to feel at home in your host country. Only then, you learn that your friends are returning to their home country or moving to another country. It can be upsetting to find out that your friends are moving. It is especially bad if you have to say goodbye to a lot of friends. Sadly most people only live abroad for a little while. After your friends leave you might miss them a lot. You might also wonder whether you will ever see them again.

Name: Caroline
Age: 10
From: United States
Lives in: Sri Lanka
Used to live in: Mali

"My friend Elise and I met when we were both living in Mali. We met in the middle of the second semester of the first grade. One of the many reasons we became friends was because we had many similar hobbies. For example, we both speak fluent French and we both love acting and things like that.

Elise and I were very good friends all through first grade. In the second grade I met Charlotte, Elise's little sister, and we became friends too. Then in third grade, Elise and Charlotte moved to Sri Lanka. I knew that I was really going to miss them. I also thought that I was never going to see them again.

I was really sad because I lost two of my closest friends. I was barely eight then and it would've been hard to stay in touch because my e-mail skills were limited. To my great surprise we were reunited a year later in fourth grade.

I will always remember when I saw Elise for the first time in Sri Lanka. She was in physical education class and my family and I were on a tour of the school. I remember that it gave me a really happy and reassuring feeling to know that there was a friendly face. It was great to have a friend to help me learn about my new school and find my way around. Since then we've been together and now we're both in fifth grade.

The point of this story is that it's a small world after all. I mean that amazing coincidences do sometimes happen to people who live abroad. Take for example what happened to me. Even if it doesn't happen to you, don't worry. In my experience of living abroad, I've had to make new friends a lot. I've had wonderful friends in every country I've lived in."

Name: Allison
Age: 10
From: United States
Lives in: Colombia
Used to live in: El Salvador

"One day my mom told me she got her bid list. I didn't know what a bid list was and so I asked. Mom said it was a list to see where we will be going next. I couldn't believe that my first post was over. It felt strange to be moving and depressing to think about leaving El Salvador.

I asked my mom if we could go to Australia. She asked why I wanted to go there. I said because they speak English. At this point I was so tired of speaking Spanish. I wanted to live somewhere where I could speak English. Mom said that we would have to wait and see. Then I went off to play with my friend Beth because she had spent the night. For a little while, I forgot about the whole thing.

As the year went on, it grew closer to the time to leave. Sometimes at night, I would cry. I wasn't ready to leave El Salvador. I wasn't ready to go to a new school. I definitely wasn't ready to leave my friends. Thinking about moving to our new post in Colombia made me scared. I didn't want to be the new girl again.

Time went by fast. Before I knew it our time in El Salvador was over and it was time to go. I had to say goodbye to my best friends Beth and Becca. It was really hard. It broke my heart into pieces. As the plane took off I looked back with a tear in my eye. It was the very last time I saw El Salvador."

Name: Caroline
Age: 13
From: United States
Lives in: United Kingdom
Used to live in: Germany and Hong Kong

"For almost all of my life, I have lived in places that are not my home. I still say the hardest part is not the actual move, but saying goodbye to friends that leave every year like clockwork. In a way I am lucky, because we're not a family that lives in a place for a year and moves on. I do have the time to make friends, though it has always been rare to have more than three years with them before one of us leaves.

I didn't notice how often people leave until the fourth grade, when my friend happened to be the one leaving. That was when I realized that I couldn't go on having just one friend. I learned that I couldn't count on one person to always be there. It took me an extremely long time to get over the loss of Antonia. I found myself living for the letters and little packages she would send.

About a month after Antonia left I made six new friends. Within half a year our group went down to five when Lauren left to go back to England. At the end of that year, I was the one leaving and my friends were the ones left behind. I knew I would miss them, but I was ready for a change.

I was sick of seeing everyone come and go when I had to stay. I was tired of crying my eyes out every time I lost a friend. I knew there would be people who left wherever I went. All I could hope was that my new school in England had a smaller turnover than my old school in Germany. Now, after having lived in England for two years, I know that some things never change.

Since I came to England, I've had to say goodbye to six great friends; among them was my best friend, Katie. Saying goodbye is never easy because it feels like a part of your heart is missing. I have kept in touch with every single one of my friends since the second grade. I'm never without someone to talk to. I know that whenever I need them, I have countless friends ready to take my call."

Migrating Season: Saying Goodbye to Friends Q&A

How do I say goodbye?

By showing that you care about them and by letting them know that you are sorry that they are leaving. Saying goodbye is tough. It's especially hard when you have to do it all the time. After a while you might act as though you don't really care. However when it comes to friends, it's better to be honest. Tell your friends that you're going to miss them. You also can show them that you care by throwing them a goodbye party.

Will I see them again?

Maybe! Just because your friends are leaving doesn't mean that you will never see them again. After all, you never know when your paths will cross again. One way to increase the odds is by staying in touch. Make sure your friends have your contact information. That way they can send you their new address.

Does it get easier?

Not really. No matter how many times you have said goodbye, it is always hard. After all, every person and every friendship is special. Each time a friend leaves, an empty space is left behind that no one else can fill. The pain eventually fades though. After a while happy memories, not sadness, will come to mind.

REAL LIFE TIP
Don't give up on friendship just because people leave. While losing friends hurts, not having friends is worse. Just think about all the things you would miss.

Moving Schmoving, Here We Go Again!

Some families do not move just once, but many times. There are several reasons for this. One reason is that a parent has a job that transfers every few years. Some children know in advance that they will be moving again. Others are surprised when they find out about yet another move. Moving again means leaving behind all that has become familiar. It also means starting over and readjusting again. It takes some time to get used to yet another country. Luckily, you already have at least one move under your belt. Your prior relocation experience can guide you during the move. It will help ensure a smooth transition, even if you are not happy about it.

Name: Aiden
Age: 8
From: United States
Lives in: Bangladesh
Used to live in: Bulgaria

"I moved to another country. First I was in Bulgaria. Then I was in the United States. Finally I moved to Bangladesh. I was so excited at the airport. I was about to go to London then Dhaka: my new home. I got on the airplane and it was really fun. Then I got to London. After I arrived I couldn't think about anything else. I just wanted to go to Bangladesh so badly.

We had the opportunity to go on an earlier flight. I didn't want to because there were lots of cool places at the airport. When I finally got on the airplane, I was so happy. Then I figured out that it wasn't going to be that much fun. After all it was going to take like five million hours. I started bugging my mom about everything and didn't go to sleep the whole night.

When I got to Dhaka I was just so happy that I was finally in my new home. I was also happy because I had stayed up for a whole day and a whole night and would finally be able to go to sleep. I looked out the window of the car as we drove to our new house in Dhaka. I saw all these busted up cars and stuff and I thought that Dhaka was going to be a busted up place.

During the orientation at my new school I looked around and realized that it was actually a lot better than my old school in Bulgaria. The school in Dhaka had a better playground and better stuff. I was so tired that day that I actually fell asleep on my feet right there in the school. My dad woke me up.

Now that we are here, we love it. We like it so much that we have extended our stay for a third year. We might even extend it by another year. I hope we will!"

Name: Loic
Age: 10
From: United States
Lives in: Morrocco
Used to live in: Australia, Niger, and Uganda

"When it's time to go to another post, my mom and dad do some research. My mom finds schools in different countries. My dad checks that his new job is a great job. Next my mom and dad ask us if we want to go to a certain country. When that happens, my sister and I know what to do. We get out the globe and find out where the country is. Then we ask our mom and dad lots of questions.

I don't like moving this much. It's hard to leave every two or three years. I get better and better at it each time we do it. I still don't like it. I don't like making new friends and then leaving them. It's hard and very, very sad. We always try to stay in touch and sometimes it's okay. Usually it's hard and sad.

Moving to yet another country is annoying, hard, and irritating. It takes me two to three years to get used to a country. By the time I am used to it, we leave. That is one reason I don't like it. It's irritating. Another reason is that I like soccer. Some countries like soccer too. Others don't. When that happens I don't get to play soccer.

Preparing for a new country is like preparing for a new world. It's like getting ready for a new life and a new dimension. When I move to another country, I end one life and begin a new one. To me, life is like a jigsaw puzzle. You need all the right pieces to end it correctly. In my case, I have all the different pieces, but still need to put them together correctly."

Name: Selengei
Age: 11
From: United States
Lives in: Norway
Used to live in: Kenya

"I used to live in Kenya. I was even born there. Even though I used to live in Africa, I'm not black. I'm white. My mother is from the United States but has lived in Kenya for most of her life. My father is from Norway. We have family in Kenya, the United States, and Norway.

One day my mom and dad decided to tell me that we were moving to Norway. I was very sad and very furious. I told them that I wasn't going to go. I ran out of the house and climbed up a tree. I stayed up there for a while. My mom was also sad. She was sad because I was sad. I went to her.

I know what to expect about life in Norway. I've been there lots of times. I like Norway, but it'll never be my home. Kenya will always be my home. We'll go back twice a year. That makes it a little better. In Kenya, there are so many different animals. In Norway there are so few. I will miss all the animals.

My mom and dad study elephants. I've spent a lot of time with wild animals. When the elephants speak my mom can understand them. My parents work in Amboseli National Park at the base of Kilimanjaro. When we go to the field site, we live in tents and are surrounded by wild animals.

Kenya and Norway are very different. At home in Kenya we have a big house and wild animals in the backyard. At night we can hear the baboons calling "leopard, leopard!!" They don't say it in English, but in baboonish. Next year my Kenyan school class might come to Norway. They're going to visit some pen pals in Norway. I will go too. It'll be great to show them around and have them come to stay."

Moving Schmoving, Here We Go Again! Q&A

Why are we moving again?
It depends. There are many reasons why people move to yet another country. Some move because they are being transferred for work and will continue to

move from one international assignment to the next. Others leave because they do not like the country they are living in. Still others go because they want to further broaden their horizon. Ask your parents why you are moving again. Once you find out the reason, it will be easier to understand the move.

What if I don't want to go?

Tell your parents! While it will probably not change their minds, your parents should know how you feel. There are lots of reasons why you might not want to move again. Perhaps you are worried that you won't like your new country. Or maybe you are concerned that you will miss your old country. Once you share your feelings, your parents will be able to help you get through the move together.

Will I ever get used to this?

Not really. No matter how many times you have done it before, you must be brave to venture into an unfamiliar country. It will always be tough. And while it is adventurous, it is also a little scary. One of the good things about having moved to another country before is that you are experienced. Because of the previous experience, you know that while things may be difficult at first, eventually they will be just fine.

> **REAL LIFE TIP**
> Focus on the future. Once you move, look forward rather than back. Don't dwell on what you left behind, instead focus on what you have gained!

Identity Crisis at Age 13?
Repatriating

Repatriating, or going back home, might sound like a piece of cake. Surprisingly, moving back home can be harder than moving abroad in the first place. You have to say goodbye to your friends again. You also have to say goodbye to your house, your school, and the country you have grown to love. You do not know whether you will ever be back. Once back home, everything feels different. You may feel as if your own country is a foreign place. On the outside, you appear to blend right in. However, on the inside you wonder whether you will ever belong anywhere. This experience is so common that there is even a name for it. It is called "reverse culture shock."

Name: Phoebe
Age: 11
From: United States
Used to live in: Italy

"Moving to a new place is hard. Moving away from that new place is even harder. I had to go through it when I first moved to Italy and then moved away from Italy. I should start at the beginning. When I moved to Italy, I was really nervous because I was afraid I wouldn't make any friends. I did and we were practically inseparable. Then my mom and dad dropped the bomb that we were going to move back to the United States.

I went and told my friends. We were all heartbroken. Luckily I got to have another few precious months with my friends. Those months went by fast. The last day of school came way too quickly. It was really hard for me to say goodbye to all the friends that had been with me since the beginning. Before I knew it, I was on a plane home. My stomach had butterflies in it and my mind was about to explode. I kept wondering about the people, my new school, and my new house.

When the plane finally landed, my stomach was churning, and I was very anxious. We collected our baggage, climbed off the plane, and greeted my grandparents who were waiting. Our family drove to our new home where we were greeted by nothing but an empty house. The next day the boxes arrived and we began unpacking. I didn't know that I had so much junk. We unpacked and unpacked and unpacked until I could only see empty boxes.

Then it was time for school to begin. This was the time that I had been waiting for. The first day of school was a little scary. I didn't know anybody in my class but made a couple of friends. All in all, moving back was hard, but nothing that I couldn't handle. Living in Italy was a great experience and I'm happy that my parents made us go. I'd totally do it again."

Name: Majeda
Age: 11
From: Oman
Used to live in: United States

"I've lived in California for almost my whole life. It's a very nice place. I moved there when I was three. I went to kindergarten, first grade, second grade, and sixth grade in California. When I first came back to Oman I was seven years old. Then three years later, we moved back to California. This was because my dad wanted to finish his P.H.D. in Economics. My dad didn't want to go by himself and so we all moved.

After one year we went back to Oman. I was very excited when I heard the news. I was also a bit afraid. I didn't know what to say or do when I saw my family again. I knew that once back in Oman I would be talking about how much I missed California. I didn't want to admit this while I was still there.

Now I'm back in Oman. When I first got back I was really excited to be back in my country again. I was also sort of sad because a person who was really important to me was gone. It was my dear aunt. She had died in a car crash. At the airport, it was really emotional. All my relatives greeted us with eyes full of tears.

I really miss living in California now. I used to have so much fun while I was there. I miss everything I was able to do there as well as the celebrations and holidays. The one I liked most was Halloween. I would dress up and at night my dad would take us trick or treating. I miss everything about California right about now."

Name: Katie
Age: 12
From: Australia
Lives in: Norway
Used to live in: Canada and the United Kingdom

"I've moved from Australia to a different country three times. Every time has been a different and new experience. The first time I moved country was to Canada. We moved to a little town called St Pierre, Manitoba. We went there because my mom and dad are high school teachers. My little sister Jacqui cried when we were told that we were moving.

The biggest change about moving to Canada was the climate. There was snow at Christmas. We learned to skate and ski and built snow caves. Later we moved back to Australia. It was a 24-hour plane trip. Going back was harder than I thought it would be. Everything had changed without me. I had to remake friends and I didn't know what was going on.

Then we moved to England. We lived in a place called North Walsham, Norfolk. Starting a new school wasn't such a big deal. I had moved three times in the last three years. The new thing we tried in England was swimming in a club. We swam three nights a week every week. It was fun.

We are in Norway now. We moved here straight from England. We live in a town called Sandefjord. I go to an English speaking school and mom and dad teach at the international school. We're very happy here. The hardest thing about living here is learning the language. I'm learning it at school. I'm the only one in my class that doesn't speak fluent Norsk. We're planning to go back to Australia after this school year. I'm looking forward to it. I've enjoyed moving around the world and would encourage anyone to give it a try!"

Identity Crisis at Age 13?
Repatriating Q&A

Why does everything feel so strange?

Because you have been gone for awhile. While you were gone, parts of your former life have changed. Other things have not changed, yet still feel strange because you have changed. Living abroad has given you a new perspective. You no longer see things the way you used to see them. You have returned home with a new vision of the world. You now see old things in shiny new ways.

Will I ever fit in again?

Yes and no. The good news is that the initial "everything feels funky" phase passes. The bad news is that you likely always will feel somewhat different. Fortunately, this is not as bad as it sounds. Your experiences abroad have made you who you are. Other children have not experienced the same things. Therefore they may not understand what you are talking about. And while you may not always see eye to eye, it does not mean that you can not be friends.

What should I do with my experiences?

Share them. Many kids will have never even visited another country, let alone lived there. By telling others about your adventures, you both win. They get to hear about life in other parts of the world and you get to share your experiences. Perhaps you can hold a presentation at school or bring a special object to show-and-tell. You can also talk about your experiences with a special friend.

> **REAL LIFE TIP**
> Take some time to reminisce. Keep your memories alive by talking about them with your parents and siblings. Spend some time browsing through photo albums or even watching home movies. It is the next best thing to actually being there!

Blessings in Disguise. Reflecting on the Experience

When you first move back home, the memories, the sights, the smells and the tastes of your life abroad are still vivid. After a while, some things may become blurry. However no matter how much you forget, your life abroad and the affection for your host country will be part of you forever. The experiences and challenges are all part of your story and have made you unique. Looking back on the experience reminds you of your great adventure. You have done so much!! You have developed a greater understanding of the world and its peoples, experienced history firsthand, and explored amazing places. Life overseas sometimes seems like a bizarre movie, yet you can be proud of all you have accomplished. You are a citizen of the world!!

Name: Corey
Age: 10
From: New Zealand and Wales
Lives in: Norway
Used to live in: China

"When people ask me where I'm from, I am unable to answer. If I were a dog, you could call me a mongrel, I guess. My mother is from New Zealand and my dad is from Wales. I was born in Wales. When I was 14 months old, I moved to New Zealand. Since then I have lived in China and now in Norway.

One of the sad things about leaving was saying goodbye to my friends. I still keep in touch with them by e-mail, phone, and mail. The most annoying thing about moving was helping my parents pack and unpack. It would be helpful if my parents could get family to help with the move. Because we live far away, we don't have family support.

When I was living in China we lived on a compound. I liked living there. I also liked having an *ayi*. My parent's didn't have to do all the housework and we could spend more time together. Every Saturday we would visit a really nice hotel in Shanghai. Two things I didn't like about China were the smells and the pollution. I didn't see a blue sky for three years.

Moving from China to Norway wasn't so scary. I had lived in China long enough and wanted to move. I was just so excited to experience somewhere else to live. Norway is a very clean country and we get to see lots of blue skies. Last winter I touched snow for the first time. I also had the chance to try new sports such as skiing, ice skating, and sleighing.

I feel settled here and at the moment Norway is my home. If we were to move again I would be very upset and scared. I'm very happy here. The older I get the more difficult it is to relocate. This is because I have more friends and more memories. New Zealand is a distant memory to me now."

Name: Byron
Age: 11
From: United States
Lives in: Paraguay
Used to live in: Japan and Germany

"It's a bit hard for me to think about the past. Looking back on my overseas experience fills me with different emotions. I have many happy memories that I could share, but I also have a few sad ones. My overseas journey began when I was only three years old. I don't remember much about the move to Japan. I do remember that we moved towards the end of October.

I remember that clearly because we moved two weeks before my fourth birthday, which is also Halloween. I cried to my parents that I wouldn't have a birthday party or a costume to wear, but all was solved in no time. My parents found me a karate outfit like Bruce Lee used to wear. My mom said that I was the cutest karate kid in town.

Living in Japan was a great adventure. I was surprised to meet kids from all over the United States. I was also happy to know that I was not the only one who left at such an early age. Another great thing that came out of living in Japan is that my younger sister and brother were both born there. We are all Americans, but they were born somewhere exotic.

We ended up living in Japan for six years. Saying goodbye wasn't easy. My friends and I just used to say "*sayonara* alligator." From Japan, we moved to Germany. Life in Germany was great. I made friends from all over the world. I met kids that came from as far away as India. Learning to speak German was an adventure in itself, but I am glad I did. Then it was time to leave again. We left Germany after a year and a half with another addition to our family. It was a poodle named Peanut. He's the cutest little dog you will ever see.

The time came again to say our goodbyes. This time I said "*Tschussy* alligator." Leaving Germany wasn't easy. I still remember my sister looking out the window of the airplane waiving to the city below with tears in her eyes. Then we were off to a new adventure, this time in South America. We will be in Paraguay for another year. We don't know where we are going yet. We might be going to another country or we might be going back to the United States. Either way, I know the time will come when I have to say "*Adios* Alligator" to all my new friends.

Name: Noah
Age: 11
From: United States
Used to live: Turkey and the Netherlands

"I felt like I had moved enough in my life when my parents told me we were moving again. Twice before in my life have I had to endure this pain, yet somehow moving is kind of fun. I mean, it's not that I'm just going to forget about old friends and move on. I have kept those friends while I make new friends at my new school and my neighborhood.

All of my friends, here and there, think that I must be lonely all of the time because I keep moving. Yet everywhere I go I get less lonely. Why? Well, because everywhere I go I make new friends. I have so many friends that if I keep it up long enough, I would know everyone on this planet. Moving can also be good for school. At my new school, my reports on other countries are very good and my geography is very good as well.

Looking back is very important. It teaches you to try harder in the country you are living in now. If you didn't explore your neighborhood enough, then try to do that in this new country. I very much regret not getting to know my Dutch neighbors well enough. I plan to do this back home in the United States now that I've returned from Holland."

Blessings in Disguise.
Reflecting on the Experience Q&A

What if I forget things?

It's okay. While you might want to remember everything about your former life abroad, it is likely that you won't. After all, even remembering everything that happened yesterday is challenging. Just because you forget things, does not mean that the experience was not special. Your life abroad will stay with you forever.

Why does no one care?

Because they did not experience it for themselves and find it hard to relate to your experiences. The experience of living abroad was amazing to you. Other children do not know what it is like to live in another country. They may not have even heard of the places that you called home. Sometimes kids may think you are bragging, when you feel that you are just talking about life. Probably they just do not understand.

What happens next?

No one knows. Your parents might decide to stay put or they might decide to move again. Talk to them to find out what their plans are. Once you are an adult, you will decide where to live. You might decide to live in your own country. You might also decide to study or work abroad. The choice is yours!

> **REAL LIFE TIP**
> Live in the present. Don't just survive, thrive!!! No matter where in the world you live, life can throw you a curve ball and you can still hit a home run. Whether at home or overseas, seek out your adventures. There is, after all, no time like the present!

About the Author

Born and raised in the Netherlands, Martine Zoer imagined what it would be like to live in another country. At the age of sixteen, she began spending her summers working abroad. After graduating from high school, Martine studied journalism, longing to live a life to inspire her writing. After college, she moved and lived in the United Kingdom, the United States and Canada. Martine's first book, *WereldKIDS*, was published in 2003. In the book, Dutch children share their experiences of life abroad and offer practical advice for children living and moving abroad. Rave reviews and acclamations inspired Martine to write The Kids' Guide to Living Abroad so that all children living abroad can benefit from the experiences of others. Martine is interested in writing books for children by children because she believes such books encourage children to handle the struggles of global transitions confidently and also benefit from their experiences. Currently, Martine is a writer and expatriate living in San Francisco.

About the Illustrator

Michelle Christensen's parents were in the American Foreign Service. So like the children in this book, Michelle lived internationally for most of her youth. She spent 14 years of her childhood living in Taiwan, Beijing, Hong Kong, and South Africa. Illustrating the Kids' Guide to Living Abroad brought back memories for Michelle who relates to the experiences of the children living internationally mobile lifestyles. Reflecting on her experience, Michelle believes that while growing up abroad was challenging, it was enriching and she would not trade it for anything. At the young age of three, a lifelong passion for art was sparked. Michelle was determined to succeed as an artist. To fulfill her dream, Michelle currently studies illustration at Brigham Young University. When she is not studying, she works side jobs illustrating for different companies and websites. She also enjoys her greeting card and jewelry business.